Chiang Mai & Northern Thailand

Andrew Spooner

Credits

Footprint credits

Editor: Felicity Laughton
Production and layout: Emma Bryers
Maps: Kevin Feeney
Cover: Pepi Bluck

Publisher: Patrick Dawson
Managing Editor: Felicity Laughton
Advertising: Elizabeth Taylor
Sales and marketing: Kirsty Holmes

Photography credits
Front cover: Shutterstock/Ataki
Back cover: Shutterstock/nofilm2011

Printed in Great Britain by CPI Antony Rowe, Chippenham, Wiltshire

Publishing information

Footprint *Focus Chiang Mai & Northern Thailand*
2nd edition
© Footprint Handbooks Ltd
September 2013

ISBN: 978 1 909268 51 7
CIP DATA: A catalogue record for this book is available from the British Library

® Footprint Handbooks and the Footprint mark are a registered trademark of Footprint Handbooks Ltd

Published by Footprint
6 Riverside Court
Lower Bristol Road
Bath BA2 3DZ, UK
T +44 (0)1225 469141
F +44 (0)1225 469461
footprinttravelguides.com

Distributed in the USA by Globe Pequot Press, Guilford, Connecticut

The content of Footprint *Focus Chiang Mai & Northern Thailand* has been taken directly from Footprint's *Thailand Handbook* which was researched and written by Andrew Spooner.

Contents

It begins with an easing of the dusty, overwhelming heat of the plains. Limestone hills draped with calming verdant forest, roads and rivers twisting into endless switchbacks. The air seems cleaner, the people and pace gentler. After the raucous intensity of most of the rest of Thailand, the north feels like another country; factor in the diverse array of the tribal hill peoples, and in many respects it is.

The north wasn't incorporated into the Thai nation until the beginning of the 20th century. For centuries local lords held sway over shifting principalities, the most significant being centred on Chiang Mai. This city remains the largest in the north, and a magnet for thousands of tourists. With its walled centre, serene and ancient temples, bustling markets and excellent accommodation it's easy to understand why.

Travel to the west of Chiang Mai and you'll find beautiful Mae Hong Son, encircled by hills and often cloaked in mist. En route take in Pai; set in a stunning location this is a travellers' hang-out with all the banana pancakes you could ever consume. Head upcountry and you'll reach the venerable city of Chiang Rai, an important trekking centre. Most of its history has been lost but Chiang Rai is still a friendly and proud place. With the opening up of Burma and routes into China, the far north is slowly emerging as an important trading route. Mae Sai, which offers the opportunity for excursions into Burma, is a bustling market town, whilst Chiang Khong, on the Mekong, is a crossing point into Laos. The 14th-century fortified *wiang* (walled city) of Chiang Saen is now an important Mekong river port and just north of there is the infamous Golden Triangle, where Laos, Burma and Thailand meet. Finally, some of Thailand's most beautiful and peaceful monasteries are found in the north. Wat Phra Singh in Chiang Mai, Wat Phumin in Nan and, perhaps the finest of them, Wat Phra That Lampang Luang, in Lampang, is an extraordinary display of temple craft.

Planning your trip

Getting to Thailand

Air

The majority of visitors arrive in Thailand through Bangkok's **Suvarnabhumi International Airport**. A number of budget airlines fly domestic routes from the city's old airport, Don Muang. Chiang Mai in the north and Phuket in the south also have international airports. More than 35 airlines and charter companies fly to Bangkok. **THAI** is the national carrier. Fares inflate by up to 50% during high season.

Flights from Europe The approximate flight time from London to Bangkok (non-stop) is 12 hours. From London Heathrow, airlines offering non-stop flights include **Qantas**, **British Airways**, **THAI** and **Eva Air**. You can easily connect to Thailand from the UK via most other European capitals. **Finnair** flies daily from Helsinki, **KLM** via Amsterdam and **Lufthansa** via Frankfurt. **SAS** flies from Copenhagen and **Swiss Air** from Zurich. Further afield, **Etihad** flies via Abu Dhabi, **Gulf Air** via Bahrain and **Qatar** via Muscat and Doha. Non-direct flights can work out much cheaper, so if you want a bargain, shop around. **Finnair**, www.finnair.com, often offers some of the cheapest fares. It is also possible to fly direct to Chiang Mai from Dusseldorf, Frankfurt and Munich in Germany, and to Phuket from Dusseldorf and Munich.

Flights from the USA and Canada The approximate flight time from Los Angeles to Bangkok is 21 hours. There are one-stop flights from Los Angeles on **THAI** and two-stops on **Delta**; one-stop flights from San Francisco on **Northwest** and **United** and two-stops on **Delta**; and one-stop flights from Vancouver on **Canadian**. **THAI** have now started a non-stop flight from New York to Bangkok, which takes 16 hours.

Flights from Australasia There are flights from Sydney and Melbourne (approximately nine hours) daily with **Qantas** and **THAI**. There is also a choice of other flights with **British Airways**, **Alitalia**, **Lufthansa** and **Lauda Air**, which are less frequent. There are flights from Perth with **THAI** and **Qantas**. From Auckland, **Air New Zealand**, **THAI** and **British Airways** fly to Bangkok.

Flights from Asia THAI, **Air India** and **Indian Airlines**, SriLankan Airlines and **Cathay Pacific** fly from Colombo to Bangkok. From Dhaka, there are flights with **Biman Bangladesh Airlines** and **THAI**. PIA and **THAI** fly from Karachi. **Royal Nepal Airlines** and **THAI** fly from Kathmandu. It is also possible to fly to Chiang Mai from Kunming (China) and Singapore and to Phuket from Hong Kong, Kuala Lumpur, Penang, Singapore, Taipei and Tokyo. Numerous airlines fly from Hong Kong, Tokyo, Manila, Kuala Lumpur, Singapore and Jakarta to Bangkok. There are daily connections from Singapore and Kuala Lumpur to Hat Yai and from Singapore and Hong Kong to Koh Samui. It is also possible to fly to Phuket from Hong Kong, Kuala Lumpur, Penang, Singapore, Taipei and Tokyo.

There has been a massive proliferation of budget airlines in Southeast Asia with Bangkok becoming one of the primary hubs. There are cheap fares available to/from Laos, Cambodia, Singapore, China, Macau, Maldives, Hong Kong and Malaysia. The pick of the bunch is Air Asia (www.airasia.com) which runs various routes to neighbouring countries. Bangkok has

Don't miss...

Numbers relate to the map on page 4.

a concentration of tour companies specializing in Indochina and Burma and is a good place to arrange a visa (although most of these countries now issue visas on arrival).

Flights from the Middle East Etihad, flies from Abu Dhabi, **Gulf Air** flies from Bahrain, and **Egyptair** from Cairo.

Transport in Chiang Mai and Northern Thailand

The quickest way of getting to Chiang Mai is by air. A number of airlines offer flights from Bangkok as well as links to other provincial centres. The airport, www.chiangmai airportonline.com, is 3 km southwest of town, call T053-270222 for airport information. Banks, currency exchange, hotel booking counters, car rental counters and airport information are all at hand in the Arrivals area. Taxis into town cost about ฿100-150 and can be arranged at the taxi booking counter.

There are several trains a day from Bangkok (12 hours) including the splendid sleeper service. 'Special Express' trains with first-class and second-class sleeper berths depart Bangkok at 1810 and 1935 and arrive in Chiang Mai at 0745 and 0945 respectively. The later 'Express', departing Bangkok at 2200 and arriving in Chiang Mai at 1245, offers second-class berths. Over recent years the railway connecting Bangkok and Chiang Mai has suffered a number of minor accidents and the line badly needs investment. The government has planned a high-speed train route to connect Bangkok and the north but it may be a number of years before this is complete. For more information on trains from Bangkok, visit www.railway.co.th. The station is in the east of the town, on Charoen Muang Road, across the Ping River. To get to town, there are frequent *songthaews* and tuk-tuks.

Scores of buses arrive from all over Thailand – from super-luxury VIP buses through to the bone-shaking ordinary variety. The long-distance bus station is at the Chiang Mai Arcade, on the corner of the super highway and Kaew Nawarat Road, northeast of town, T053-242664. Tuk-tuks and *songthaews* wait at the station to take passengers into town. ▸▸ *See Transport, page 58.*

Where to stay in Chiang Mai and Northern Thailand

Thailand has a large selection of hotels, including some of the best in the world. Standards outside of the usual tourist areas have improved immensely over recent years and while such places might not be geared to Western tastes they offer some of the best-value accommodation in the country. Due to its popularity with backpackers, Thailand also has many small guesthouses, serving Western food and catering to the foibles of foreigners. These are concentrated in the main tourist areas.

Hotels and guesthouses

Hotels and guesthouses are listed under eight categories, according to the average price of a double/twin room for one night. It should be noted that many hotels will have a range of rooms, some with air conditioning (a/c) and attached bathroom facilities, others with just a fan and shared facilities. Prices can therefore vary a great deal. If a hotel entry lists 'some a/c', then these rooms are likely to be in the upper part of the range, perhaps even in the next range. Few hotels in Thailand provide breakfast in the price of the room. A service charge of 10% and government tax of 7% will usually be added to the bill in the more expensive hotels (categories $$$$-$$). Ask whether the quoted price includes tax when checking in. Prices in Bangkok are inflated.

During the off-season, hotels and guesthouses in tourist destinations may halve their room rates so it is always worthwhile bargaining or asking whether there is a special price. Given the fierce competition among hotels, it is even worth trying during the peak season. Over-building has meant that there is a glut of rooms in some towns and hotels are desperate for business.

Until 10 years ago, most guesthouses offered shared facilities with cold-water showers and squat toilets. Levels of cleanliness were also less than pristine. Nowadays, Western toilet imperialism is making inroads into Thai culture and many of the better-run guesthouses will have good, clean toilets with sit-down facilities and, sometimes, hot water. Some are even quite stylish in their bathroom facilities. Fans are the norm in most guesthouses although, again, to cash in on the buying power of backpackers with more disposable income more and more offer air-conditioned rooms as well. Check that mosquito nets are provided.

Security is a problem, particularly in beach resort areas where flimsy bungalows offer easy access to thieves. Keep valuables with the office for safekeeping (although there are regular cases of people losing valuables that have been left in 'safekeeping') or on your person when you go out. Guesthouses can be tremendous value for money. With limited overheads, family labour and using local foods they can cut their rates in a way that larger hotels with armies of staff, imported food and expensive facilities simply cannot.

Camping and national park accommodation

It is possible to camp in Thailand and **national parks** are becoming much better at providing campsites and associated facilities. Most parks will have public toilets with basic facilities. Some parks also offer bungalows; these fall into our **$$** accommodation category but because they can often accommodate large groups their per person cost is less than this. The more popular parks will often also have privately run accommodation including sophisticated resorts, sometimes within the park boundaries. For reservations at any of the national parks contact: **Reservation Office** ① *National Parks Division, Royal Forestry Department, 61 Phanhonyothin Rd, Ladyao, Jatujak, Bangkok, T02-56142923. The official*

Price codes

Where to stay

$$$$ over US$100 $$$ US$46-100

$$ US$20-45 $ under US$20

Prices include taxes and service charge, but not meals. They are based on a double room, except in the $ range, where prices are almost always per person.

Restaurants

$$$ over US$12 $$ US$6-12 $ under US$6

Prices refer to the cost of an average main dish. They do not include drinks.

website, www.dnp.go.th/parkreserve, is excellent for making online bookings. Alternatively, you can phone the park offices listed in the relevant sections of this guide. **Beaches** are considered public property – anybody can camp on them for free.

In terms of what to bring and wear, bear in mind that at night at high elevations, even in muggy Thailand, it can be cold. In the north and northeast it can fall to close to freezing during the cooler months. During the day, long trousers (to avoid scratches), sturdy shoes (if you are thinking of trekking any distance), and a hat are recommended. In the evening, long-sleeved shirts (to keep the mosquitoes at bay) are required. If you are camping, remember that while the more popular parks have tents for hire, the rest – and this means most – do not. Bring your own torch, camp stove, fuel and toilet paper.

Food and drink in Chiang Mai and Northern Thailand

Thai food, for long an exotic cuisine distant from the average northerner's mind and tongue, has become an international success story. The Thai government, recognizing the marketing potential of their food, has instituted a plan called 'Global Thai' to boost the profile of Thai food worldwide as a means of attracting more people to visit its country of origin. Thai food has become, in short, one of Thailand's most effective advertisements.

Thai food is an intermingling of Tai, Chinese and, to a lesser extent, Indian cuisines. This helps to explain why restaurants produce dishes that must be some of the (spicy) hottest in the world, as well as others that are rather bland. *Larb* (traditionally raw – but now more frequently cooked – chopped beef mixed with rice, herbs and spices) is a traditional 'Tai' dish; *pla priaw waan* (whole fish with soy and ginger) is Chinese in origin; while *gaeng mussaman* (beef 'Muslim' curry) was brought to Thailand by Muslim immigrants. Even satay, paraded by most restaurants as a Thai dish, was introduced from Malaysia and Indonesia (which themselves adopted it from Arab traders during the Middle Ages).

Despite these various influences, Thai cooking is distinctive. Thais have managed to combine the best of each tradition, adapting elements to fit their own preferences. Remarkably, considering how ubiquitous it is in Thai cooking, the chilli pepper is a New World fruit and was not introduced into Thailand until the late 16th century (along with the pineapple and the papaya).

A Thai meal is based around rice, and many wealthy Bangkokians own farms upcountry where they cultivate their favourite variety. When a Thai asks another Thai whether he has eaten he will ask, literally, whether he has 'eaten rice' (*kin khao*). Similarly, the accompanying dishes are referred to as food 'with the rice'. There are two main types of rice – 'sticky' or glutinous (*khao niaw*) and non-glutinous (*khao jao*). Sticky rice is usually used to make sweets (desserts) although it is the staple in the northeastern region and parts of the north. *Khao jao* is standard white rice.

In addition to rice, a meal usually consists of a soup like *tom yam kung* (prawn soup), *kaeng* (a curry) and *krueng kieng* (a number of side dishes). Thai food is spicy, and aromatic herbs and grasses (like lemongrass, coriander, tamarind and ginger) are used to give a distinctive flavour. *Nam pla* (fish sauce made from fermented fish and used as a condiment) and *nam prik* (*nam pla*, chillies, garlic, sugar, shrimps and lime juice) are two condiments that are taken with almost all meals. *Nam pla* is made from steeping fish, usually anchovies, in brine for long periods and then bottling the peatish-coloured liquor produced. Chillies deserve a special mention because most Thais like their food HOT! Some chillies are fairly mild; others – like the tiny, red *prik khii nuu* ('mouse shit pepper') – are fiendishly hot.

Isaan food – from the northeast of Thailand – is also distinctive, very similar to Lao cuisine and very popular. Most of the labourers and service staff come from Isaan, particularly in Bangkok, and you won't have to go far to find a rickety street stall selling sticky rice, aromatic *kai yang* (grilled chicken) and fiery *som tam* (papaya salad). *Pla ra* (fermented fish) is one of Isaan's most famous dishes but is usually found only in the most authentic Isaan dishes, its salty, pungent flavour being too much for effete Bangkokians.

Due to Thailand's large Chinese population (or at least Thais with Chinese roots), there are also many Chinese-style restaurants whose cuisine is variously 'Thai-ified'. Many of the snacks available on the streets show this mixture of Thai and Chinese, not to mention Arab and Malay. *Bah jang*, for example, are small pyramids of leaves stuffed with sticky rice, Chinese sausage, salted eggs, pork and dried shrimp. They were reputedly first created for the Chinese dragon boat festival but are now available 12 months a year – for around ฿20.

To sample Thai food it is best to go in a group to a restaurant and order a range of dishes. To eat alone is regarded as slightly strange. However, there are a number of 'one-dish' meals like fried rice and *phat thai* (fried noodles) and restaurants will also usually provide *raat khao* ('over rice'), which is a dish like a curry served on a bed of rice for a single person.

Strict non-fish-eating **vegetarians** and **vegans** are in for a tough time. Nearly every cooked meal you will eat in Thailand will be liberally doused in *nam pla* or cooked with shrimp paste. At more expensive and upmarket international restaurants you'll probably be able to find something suitable – in the rural areas, you'll be eating fruit, fried eggs and rice, though not all at once. There are a network of Taoist restaurants offering more strict veggie fare throughout the country – look out for yellow flags with red Chinese lettering. Also asking for 'mai sai nam pla' (no *nam pla*)– when ordering what should be veggie food might keep the fish sauce out of harm's reach.

Restaurants
It is possible to get a tasty and nutritious meal almost anywhere – and at any time – in Thailand. Thais eat out a great deal so that most towns have a range of places. Starting at the top, in pecuniary terms at any rate, the more sophisticated restaurants are usually air-conditioned, and sometimes attached to a hotel. In places like Bangkok and Chiang Mai they may be Western in style and atmosphere. In towns less frequented by foreigners they are likely to be rather more functional – although the food will be just as good. In addition to these more upmarket restaurants are a whole range of places from **noodle shops** to **curry houses** and **seafood restaurants**. Many small restaurants have no menus. But often the speciality of the house will be clear – roasted, honeyed ducks hanging in the window, crab and fish laid out on crushed ice outside. Away from the main tourist spots, 'Western'

breakfasts are commonly unavailable, so be prepared to eat Thai-style (noodle or rice soup or fried rice). Yet, the quality of much Thai food can be mixed, with many Thai restaurants and street stalls using huge amounts of sugar, MSG and oil in their cooking.

Towards the bottom of the scale are **stalls and food carts**. These tend to congregate at particular places in town – often in the evening, from dusk – although they can be found just about anywhere: outside the local provincial offices, along a cul-de-sac, or under a conveniently placed shady tree. Stall holders will tend to specialize in either noodles, rice dishes, fruit drinks, sweets and so on. Hot meals are usually prepared to order. While stall food may be cheap – a meal costs only around ฿25-35 – they are frequented by people from all walks of life. A well-heeled businessman in a suit is just as likely to be seen bent over a bowl of noodles at a rickety table on a busy street corner as a construction worker.

A popular innovation over the last 10 years or so has been the *suan a-haan* or **garden restaurant**. These are often on the edge of towns, with tables set in gardens, sometimes with bamboo furniture and ponds. Another type of restaurant worth a mention is the **Thai-style coffee shop**. These are sometimes attached to hotels in provincial towns and feature hostesses dressed in Imelda-esque or skimpy spangly costumes. The hostesses, when they are not crooning to the house band, sit with customers, laugh at their jokes and assiduously make sure that their glasses are always full.

In the north, *khantoke* dining is de rigueur – or so one might imagine from the number of restaurants offering it. It is a northern Thai tradition, when people sit on the floor to eat at low tables, often to the accompaniment of traditional music and dance.

Tourist centres also provide good European, American and Japanese food at reasonable prices. Bangkok boasts some superb restaurants. Less expensive Western **fast-food** restaurants can also be found, including **McDonald's** and **Kentucky Fried Chicken**.

The etiquette of eating

The Thai philosophy on eating is 'often', and most Thais will snack their way through the day. Eating is a relaxed, communal affair and it is not necessary to get too worked up about etiquette. Dishes are placed in the middle of the table where diners can help themselves. In a restaurant rice is usually spooned out by a waiter or waitress – and it is considered good manners to start a meal with a spoon of rice. While food is eaten with a spoon and fork, the fork is only used to manoeuvre food onto the spoon. Because most food is prepared in bite-sized pieces it is not usually necessary to use a knife. At noodle stalls chopsticks and china soup spoons are used while in the northeast most people – at least at home – use their fingers. Sticky rice is compressed into a ball using the ends of the fingers and then dipped in the other dishes. Thais will not pile their plates with food but take several small portions from the dishes arranged on a table. It is also considered good manners when invited out to leave some food on your plate, as well as on the serving dishes on the table. This demonstrates the generosity of the host.

Drink

Water in nearly every single restaurant and street stall now comes from large bottles of purified water but if you're unsure, buy your own.

Coffee is consumed throughout Thailand. In stalls and restaurants, coffee comes with a glass of Chinese tea. Soft drinks are widely available too. Many roadside stalls prepare fresh fruit juices in liquidizers while hotels produce all the usual cocktails.

Major brands of **spirits** are served in most hotels and bars, although not always off the tourist path. The most popular spirit among Thais is Mekhong – local cane whisky –

which can be drunk straight or with mixers such as Coca-Cola. However, due to its hangover-inducing properties, more sophisticated Thais prefer Johnny Walker or an equivalent brand.

Beer drinking is spreading fast. The most popular local beer is Singha beer brewed by Boon Rawd. Singha, Chang and Heineken are the three most popular beers in Thailand. Leo and Cheers are agreeable budget options although they are seldom sold in restaurants. Beer is relatively expensive in Thai terms as it is heavily taxed by the government. It is a high status drink, so the burgeoning middle class, especially the young, are turning to beer in preference to traditional, local whiskies – which explains why brewers are so keen to set up shop in this traditionally non-beer drinking country. Some pubs and bars also sell beer on tap – which is known as *bier sot*, 'fresh' beer.

Thais are fast developing a penchant for **wine**. Imported wines are expensive by international standards but Thailand now has six wineries, mainly in the northeastern region around Nakhon Ratchasima. For tours around the wine regions (including to a vineyard where the workers use elephants) contact Laurence Civil (laurence@csloxinfo.com).

Essentials A-Z

Accident and emergency
Emergency services Police: T191, T123. **Tourist police:** T1155. **Fire:** T199. Ambulance: T02-2551134-6. **Tourist Assistance Centre:** Rachdamnern Nok Av, Bangkok, T02-356 0655.

Calling one of the emergency numbers will not usually be very productive as few operators speak English. It is better to call the tourist police or have a hotel employee or other English-speaking Thai telephone for you. For more intractable problems contact your embassy or consulate.

Electricity
Voltage is 220 volts (50 cycles). Most 1st- and tourist-class hotels have outlets for shavers and hairdryers. Adaptors are recommended, as almost all sockets are 2-pronged.

Embassies and consulates
Thai embassies worldwide
www.thaiembassy.org is a useful resource.

Health
Hospitals/medical services are listed in the Directory sections of each chapter.

Staying healthy in Thailand is straightforward. With the following advice and precautions you should keep as healthy as you do at home. Most visitors return home having experienced no problems at all beyond an upset stomach. However, in Thailand the health risks, especially in the tropical areas, are different from those encountered in Europe or the USA. It also depends on how you travel and where. The country has a mainly tropical climate; nevertheless the acquisition of true tropical disease by the visitor is probably conditioned as much by the rural nature and standard of hygiene of the surroundings than by the climate. Malaria is common in certain areas, particularly in the jungle.

There is an obvious difference in health risks between the business traveller who tends to stay in international class hotels in the large cities and the backpacker trekking through the rural areas. There are no hard and fast rules to follow; you will often have to make your own judgement on the healthiness or otherwise of your surroundings. Check with your doctor on the status of Avian flu before you go. At the time of writing, Thailand was clear of bird flu.

Before you go
Ideally, you should see your GP/practice nurse or travel clinic at least 6 weeks before your departure for general advice on travel risks, malaria and recommended vaccinations. Your local pharmacist can also be a good source of readily accessible advice. Make sure you have travel insurance, get a dental check (especially if you are going to be away for more than a month), know your own blood group and if you suffer a long-term condition such as diabetes or epilepsy make sure someone knows or that you have a **Medic Alert** bracelet/necklace with this information on it.

Recommended vaccinations
No vaccinations are specifically required for Thailand unless coming from an infected area, but tuberculosis, rabies, Japanese B encephalitis and hepatitis B are commonly recommended. The final decision, however, should be based on a consultation with your GP or travel clinic. You should also confirm that your primary courses and boosters are up to date (diphtheria, tetanus, poliomyelitis, hepatitis A, typhoid).

A yellow fever certificate is required by visitors who have been in an infected area in the 10 days before arrival. Those without a vaccination certificate will be vaccinated and kept in quarantine for 6 days, or deported.

Useful websites

www.fitfortravel.scot.nhs.uk Fit for Travel. This site from Scotland provides a quick A-Z of vaccine and travel health advice requirements for each country.
www.nathnac.org National Travel Health Network and Centre.
www.who.int World Health Organization.

Money
Currency

Exchange rates: for up-to-the-minute exchange rates visit www.xe.com.

The unit of Thai currency is the **baht** (฿), which is divided into 100 **satang**. Notes in circulation include ฿20 (green), ฿50 (blue), ฿100 (red), ฿500 (purple) and ฿1000 (orange and grey). Coins include 25 satang and 50 satang, and ฿1, ฿2, ฿5, and ฿10. The 2 smaller coins are disappearing from circulation and the 25 satang coin, equivalent to the princely sum of US$0.003, is rarely found. The colloquial term for 25 satang is saleng.

Exchange

It is best to change money at banks or money changers which give better rates than hotels. The exchange booths at Bangkok airport have some of the best rates available. There is no black market. First-class hotels have 24-hr money changers. Indonesian rupiah, Nepalese rupees, Burmese kyat, Vietnamese dong, Lao kip and Cambodian riels cannot be exchanged for baht at Thai banks. (Money changers will sometimes exchange kyat, dong, kip and riel and it can be a good idea to buy the currencies in Bangkok before departure for these countries as the black-market rate often applies.) There is a charge of ฿23 per cheque when changing **traveller's cheques** (passport required) so it works out cheaper to travel with large denomination traveller's cheques (or avoid them altogether).

Currency cards

If you don't want to carry lots of cash, prepaid currency cards allow you to preload money from your bank account, fixed at the day's exchange rate. They look like a credit or debit card and are issued by specialist money changing companies, such as Travelex and Caxton FX. You can top up and check your balance by phone, online and sometimes by text.

Credit and debit cards

Plastic is increasingly used in Thailand and just about every town of any size will have a bank with an ATM. Visa and MasterCard are the most widely taken credit cards, and cash cards with the Cirrus logo can also be used to withdraw cash at many banks. Generally speaking, AMEX can be used at branches of the **Bangkok Bank**; JCB at **Siam Commercial Bank**; MasterCard at **Siam Commercial** and **Bangkok Bank**; and Visa at **Thai Farmers' Bank** and **Bangkok Bank**. Most larger hotels and more expensive restaurants take credit cards as well. Because Thailand has embraced the ATM with such exuberance, many foreign visitors no longer bother with traveller's cheques or cash and rely entirely on plastic. Even so, a small stash of US dollars cash can come in handy in a sticky situation.

Notification of credit card loss: **American Express**, SP Building, 388 Phahonyothin Rd, Bangkok 10400, T02-2735544; **Diners Club**, Dusit Thani Building, Rama IV Rd, T02-233 5644, T02-238 3660; **JCB**, T02-256 1361, T02-2561351; **Visa** and **MasterCard**, Thai Farmers Bank Building, Phahonyothin Rd, T02-251 6333, T02-273 1199.

Cost of living

One of the key pledges of the Yingluck Shinawatra government elected in 2011 was to increase the minimum wage to ฿300 a day (US$10). By mid-2012, despite complaints by many of the richest individuals and companies in Thailand, this was coming into force. The average salary of a civil servant is now around US$500 a month. Of course, Thailand's middle classes – and especially those engaged in business in Bangkok – will earn far more than this. Thailand has appalling wealth distribution yet Thai society is remarkably cohesive. A simple but good meal out will cost ฿60; the rental of a modern house in a provincial city will cost perhaps ฿4000 a month.

Cost of travelling
Visitors staying in the best hotels and eating in hotel restaurants could easily spend ฿5000 per day, conceivably much much more. Tourists staying in cheaper a/c accommodation and eating in local restaurants will probably spend about ฿600-900 per day. Backpackers staying in fan-cooled guesthouses and eating cheaply, should be able to live on ฿300 per day. In Bangkok, expect to pay 20-30% more.

Opening hours
Banks Mon-Fri 0830-1530. **Exchange** Daily 0830-2200 in Bangkok, Pattaya, Phuket and Chiang Mai. In other towns opening hours are usually shorter. **Government offices** Mon-Fri 0830-1200, 1300-1630. **Shops** 0830-1700, larger shops: 1000-1900 or 2100. **Tourist offices** 0830-1630.

Safety
In general, Thailand is a safe country to visit. The vast majority of visitors to Thailand will not experience any physical threat what so ever. However, there have been some widely publicized murders of foreign tourists in recent years and the country does have a very high murder rate. It is best to avoid any situation where violence can occur – what would be a simple punch-up or pushing bout in the West can quickly escalate in Thailand to extreme violence. This is mostly due to loss of face. Getting drunk with Thais can be a risky business – Westerners visiting the country for short periods won't be versed in the intricacies of Thai social interaction and may commit unwitting and terrible faux pas. A general rule of thumb if confronted with a situation is to appear conciliatory and offer a way for the other party to back out gracefully. It should be noted that even some police officers in Thailand represent a threat – at least 3 young Western travellers have been shot and murdered by drunken Thai policemen in the last few years. Confidence tricksters and touts operate particularly in more popular tourist centres. Robbery is also a threat; it ranges from pick-pocketing to the drugging (and subsequent robbing) of bus and train passengers. Watchfulness and simple common sense should be employed. Women travelling alone should be careful. Always lock hotel rooms and place valuables in a safe deposit if available (if not, take them with you).

Bribery
The way to make your way in life, for some people in Thailand, is through the strategic offering of gifts. A Chulalongkorn University report recently estimated that it 'costs' ฿10 million to become Bangkok Police Chief. Apparently this can be recouped in just 2 years of hard graft. Although bribing officials is by no means recommended, resident *farangs* report that they often resort to such gifts to avoid the time and hassle involved in filling in the forms and making the requisite visit to a police station for a minor traffic offence. As a visitor, it's best to play it straight.

Drugs and prostitution
Many prostitutes and drug dealers are in league with the police and may find it more profitable to report you than to take your custom (or they may try to do both). They receive a reward from the police, and the police in turn receive a bonus for the detective work. Note that foreigners on buses may be searched for drugs. Sentences for possession of illegal drugs vary from a fine or one year in jail for marijuana up to life imprisonment or execution for possession or smuggling of heroin. The death penalty is usually commuted.

Prisons

Thai prisons are very grim. Most foreigners are held in 2 Bangkok prisons – Khlong Prem and Bangkwang. One resident who visits overseas prisoners in jail wrote to us saying: "You cannot over-estimate the horrors! Khlong Prem has 7000 prisoners, 5 to a cell, with not enough room to stretch out, no recreation, one meal a day (an egg on Sundays) … ". One hundred prisoners in a dormitory is not uncommon, and prisoners on Death Row have waist chains and ankle fetters permanently welded on.

Tourist police

In 1982 the government set up a special arm of the police to deal with the demands of the tourist industry – the tourist police. Now, there is no important tourist destination that doesn't have a tourist police office. The Thai police have come in for a great deal of scrutiny over recent years, although most policemen are honest and only too happy to help the luckless visitor. **Tourist Police**, Bangkok, T02-2815051 or T02-2216206. Daily 0800-2400.

Traffic

Perhaps the greatest danger is from the traffic – especially if you are attempting to drive yourself. More foreign visitors are killed or injured in traffic accidents than in any other way. Thai drivers have a 'devil may care' attitude towards the highway code, and there are many horrific accidents. Be very careful when crossing the road – just because there is a pedestrian crossing, do not expect drivers to stop. Be particularly wary when driving or riding a motorcycle.

Tax

Airport tax is now included in the price of a ticket.

Time

GMT plus 7 hrs.

Tipping

Tipping is generally unnecessary. However, a 10% service charge is now expected on room, food and drinks bills in the smarter hotels as well as for any personal service. Increasingly, the more expensive restaurants add a 10% service charge; others expect a small tip.

Visas and immigration

For the latest information on visas and tourist visa exemptions, see the consular information section of the **Thai Ministry of Foreign Affairs** website, www.mfa.go.th. Having relocated from its central location on Soi Suan Plu, the immigration department that deals with tourists is now on the outskirts: Immigration Bureau, Government Complex Chaeng Wattana, B Building, Floor 2 (South Zone), Chaengwattana Rd Soi 7, Laksi, Bangkok 10210, T02-141 9889, www.immigration.co.th. Mon-Fri 0830-1200, 1300-1630, closed Sat, Sun, official hols.

For tourists from 41 countries (basically all Western countries, plus some Arabic and other Asian states – see www.mfa. go.th), Thai immigration authorities will issue a 30-day visa-exemption entry permit if you arrive by plane. If you enter at a land crossing from any neighbouring country, the permit is for 15 days.

Visas on arrival

Tourists from 28 countries (most of them developing countries) can apply for a 15-day visa on arrival at immigration checkpoints. Applicants must have an outbound (return) ticket and possess funds to meet living expenses of ฿10,000 per person or ฿20,000 per family. The application fee is ฿1000 and must be accompanied by a passport photo.

Tourist visas

These are valid for 60 days from date of entry and must be obtained from a Thai embassy before arrival in Thailand.

Visa extensions

These are obtainable from the Immigration Bureau (see above) for ฿1900. Applicants must bring 2 photocopies of their passport ID page and the page on which their tourist visa is stamped, together with a passport photograph. It is also advisable to dress neatly. Visas are issued by all Thai embassies and consulates. The length of time a visa is extended varies according to the office and the official.

Weights and measures

Thailand uses the metric system, although there are some traditional measures still in use, in particular the *rai*, which equals 0.16 ha. There are 4 *ngaan* in a *rai*. Other local measures include the krasorp (sack) which equals 25 kg and the *tang* which is 10-11 kg. However, for most purchases (for example fruit) the kg is the norm. Both kg and km are often referred to as lo – as in ki-lo.

Contents

Footprint features

Chiang Mai & Northern Thailand

Chiang Mai and around

When Reginald Le May wrote about Chiang Mai back in 1938, this was, in his view, one of the loveliest cities imaginable. Life, as they say, has moved on since then. But while old Thailand hands may worry about lost innocence, Chiang Mai is still worth visiting.

While in Chiang Mai don't forget to climb Doi Suthep, the city's revered mountain, which rises 1000 m above the city and is crowned with an important temple. Even if this temple has succumbed to money-grabbing practices, it is still a beautiful setting and worth the effort. A visit to the tribal museum, just to the north of the city centre, is essential to understanding the region's indigenous peoples while to the south rests the handsome remains of a ruined city, Wiang Kum Kam.

The city's monasteries are the most beautiful in the north; there is a rich tradition of arts and crafts, and the moated old city still gives a flavour of the past. It is the unofficial 'capital of the north', there are also some good practical reasons to base yourself here. It is an important transport hub, there is an excellent range of hotels and restaurants, the shopping is the best in the north, and there are also scores of trekking and other companies offering everything from whitewater rafting to elephant treks.

The nearby historical towns of Lamphun and Lampang provide handsome, striking temples – some say they are the best in the whole country. Both can be reached as day excursions from Chiang Mai though Lampang, with its laid-back riverside vibe, warrants a little more attention.

Arriving in Chiang Mai → *For hilltribes and trekking, see boxes, page 30 and 56, for all listings, see pages 38-60.*

Getting around

Much of the central part of the city can be easily covered on foot. *Songthaews* (converted pick-ups) operate as the main mode of public transport, ferrying people around for ฿20 per person (a useful guide to using them can be found at www.openchiangmai.com/Chiang_Mai_Color_Car_2211.html). *Songthaews* can also be used for longer journeys and day trips. The price is negotiable. Use landmarks (such as hotels, bridges, gates, etc) rather than street names as a guide for where you want to go. There are also tuk-tuks, some taxis and a good number of car, motorbike and bicycle hire companies. Tuk-tuks charge a minimum of ฿40 per trip, ฿60-120 for longer journeys.

Tourist information

TAT ⓘ *105/1 Chiang Mai-Lamphun Rd, T053-248607, http://www.tourismthailand.org/chiangmai, daily 0830-1630*, is very helpful and informative with good English spoken and a good range of maps and leaflets, including information on guesthouses and guidelines for trekking. In addition, there are also various free, tourist-oriented magazines: Chiang Mai Citylife (www.chiangmainews.com) is useful and the pick of the bunch. ►► *See What to do, page 53.*

Background

Around 1290 King Mengrai annexed the last of the Mon kingdoms at Lamphun and moved his capital from Chiang Rai to a site on the banks of the Ping River called Nopburi Sri Nakawan Ping Chiang Mai. It is said he chose the site after seeing a big mouse accompanied by four smaller mice scurry down a hole beneath a holy Bodhi tree. He made this site the heart of his Lanna kingdom.

Mengrai was a great patron of Theravada Buddhism and he brought monks from Ceylon to unify the country. Up until the 15th century, Chiang Mai flourished. As this century ended, relations with up-and-coming Ayutthaya became strained and the two kingdoms engaged in a series of wars with few gains on either side.

While Chiang Mai and Ayutthaya were busy fighting, the Burmese eventually captured the city of Chiang Mai in 1556. King Bayinnaung, who had unified Burma, took Chiang Mai after a three-day battle and the city remained a Burmese regency for 220 years. There was constant conflict during these years and by the time the Burmese succeeded in over-throwing Ayutthaya in 1767, the city of Chiang Mai was decimated and depopulated. In 1775, General Taksin united the kingdom of Thailand and a semi-autonomous prince of the Lampang Dynasty was appointed to rule the north. Chiang Mai lost its semi-independence in 1938 and came under direct rule from Bangkok.

Modern Chiang Mai

Today, Chiang Mai is the second largest city in Thailand, with a population of roughly 500,000; a thriving commercial centre as well as a favourite tourist destination. TAT estimates that 12% of Thailand's tourists travel to Chiang Mai. Its attractions to the visitor are obvious: the city has a rich and colourful history, still evident in the architecture of the city, which includes more than 300 wats; it is manageable and still relatively 'user friendly' (unlike Bangkok); it has perhaps the greatest concentration of handicraft

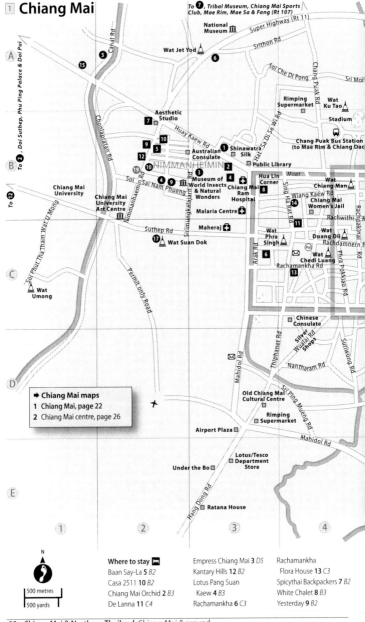

Chiang Mai

To **7**, Tribal Museum, Chiang Mai Sports Club, Mae Rim, Mae Sa & Fang (Rt 107)

National Museum

Super Highway (Rt 11)

Wat Jet Yod

Srithon Rd

Soi Che Di Pong

Chang Puak Rd

Sri Mor

Rimping Supermarket

Wat Ku Tao

Stadium

Aesthetic Studio

Huay Kaew Rd

Chang Puak Bus Station (to Mae Rim & Chiang Dac

Australian Consulate

Shinawatra Silk

NIMMANHEMIN

Public Library

Chiang Mai University

Soi Sai Nam Phueng

Museum of World Insects & Natural Wonders

Chiang Mai Ram Hospital

Hua Lin Corner

Wat Chiang Man

Chiang Mai University Art Centre

Malaria Centre

Wiang Kaew Rd

Chiang Mai Women's Jail

Maheraj

Suthep Rd

Wat Suan Dok

Wat Phra Singh

Wat Duang Di

Wat Chedi Luang

Rachamankha Rd

Wat Umong

Chinese Consulate

Silver Ware Shops

Nantharam Rd

Old Chiang Mai Cultural Centre

Rimping Supermarket

Airport Plaza

Mahidol Rd

Lotus/Tesco Department Store

Under the Bo

Hang Dong Rd

Ratana House

➡ Chiang Mai maps
1 Chiang Mai, page 22
2 Chiang Mai centre, page 26

N

500 metres
500 yards

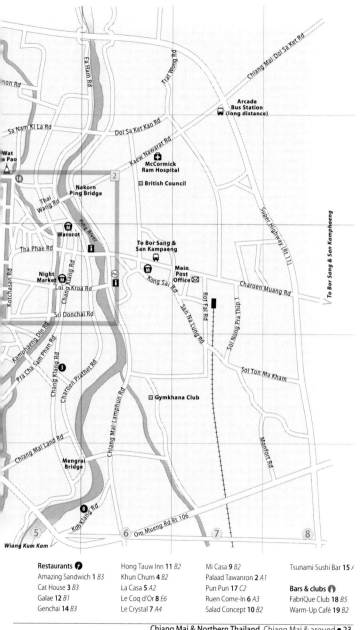

Restaurants 🍴

Amazing Sandwich **1** *B3*
Cat House **3** *B3*
Galae **12** *B1*
Genchai **14** *B3*

Hong Tauw Inn **11** *B2*
Khun Churn **4** *B2*
La Casa **5** *A2*
Le Coq d'Or **8** *E6*
Le Crystal **7** *A4*

Mi Casa **9** *B2*
Palaad Tawanron **2** *A1*
Pun Pun **17** *C2*
Ruen Come-In **6** *A3*
Salad Concept **10** *B2*

Tsunami Sushi Bar **15** *A*

Bars & clubs 🍸

FabriQue Club **18** *B5*
Warm-Up Café **19** *B2*

industries in the country; and it is also an excellent base from which to go trekking and visit the famous hilltribe villages in the surrounding highlands. Chiang Mai has developed into a major tourist centre with a good infrastructure, including excellent hotels and restaurants in all price categories. Some long-term visitors argue that the city has lost some of its charm in the process: traffic congestion, pollution and frantic property development are now much in evidence.

On a clear day at the start of the cold season, or after the rains have begun towards the end of the hot season, Chiang Mai's strategic location becomes clear. Mountains surround the city to the north, west and east, enclosing a large and rich bowl of rice fields drained by the Ping River. With Doi Suthep to the west clothed in trees and the golden *chedi* of Wat Phrathat Doi Suthep glittering on its slopes, it is a magical place.

Places in Chiang Mai → *For listings, see pages 38-60.*

Chiang Mai is centred on a square moat and defensive wall built during the 19th century. The four corner bastions are reasonably well preserved and are a useful reference point when roaming the city. Much of the rest of the town's walls were demolished during the Second World War and the bricks used for road construction. Not surprisingly, given Chiang Mai's turbulent history, many of the more important and interesting wats are within the city walls which is – surprisingly – the least built-up part. Modern commercial development has been concentrated to the east of the city and now well beyond the Ping River.

Wat Chiang Man
Situated in the northeast of the walled town, Wat Chiang Man is on Rachpakinai Road within a peaceful compound. The wat is the oldest in the city and was built by King Mengrai soon after he had chosen the site for his new capital in 1296. It is said that he resided here while waiting for his new city to be constructed and also spent the last years of his life at the monastery. The gold-topped *chedi* Chang Lom is supported by rows of elephants, similar to those of the two *chedis* of the same name at Si Satchanalai and Sukhothai. Two ancient Buddha images are contained behind bars within the *viharn*, on the right-hand side as you enter the compound. One is the crystal Buddha, Phra Sae Tang Tamani (standing 10 cm high). The second is the Phra Sila (literally, 'Stone Buddha'), believed to have originated in India or Ceylon about 2500 years ago. Wat Chiang Man is an excellent place to see how wat architecture has evolved.

Wat Pa Pao
To the northeast of Wat Chiang Man, just outside the city walls, is the unique Burmese Shan, Wat Pa Pao, which was founded more than 400 years ago by a Shan monk. A narrow *soi* leads off the busy road through an archway and into the wat's peaceful and rather ramshackle compound. The *chedi* is a melange of stuccoed animals from *singhas* to *nagas*, while the flat-roofed *viharn*, with its dark and atmospheric interior, contains three Buddha images. The monks at the wat are Shan – most having come here from Burma over the last few years – and it continues to serve Chiang Mai's Shan community.

Wat Phra Singh
Wat Phra Singh (Temple of the Lion Buddha) is situated in the west quarter of the **old city** and is impressively positioned at the end of Phra Singh Road (see map, page 22). The wat was founded in 1345 and contains a number of beautiful buildings decorated with

fine woodcarving. Towards the back of the compound is the intimate Lai Kham Viharn, which houses the venerated Phra Buddha Singh image. It was built between 1385 and 1400 and the walls are decorated with early 18th-century murals. The **Phra Buddha Sihing** is said to have come from Ceylon by a rather roundabout route but, as art historians point out, is Sukhothai in style. The head, which was stolen in 1922, is a copy. Among the other buildings in the wat is an attractive raised *hor trai* (library), with intricate carved wood decorations, inset with mother-of-pearl.

Wat Chedi Luang and city pillar

On Phra Pokklao Road, to the east of Wat Phra Singh, is the 500-year-old ruined *chedi* of Wat Chedi Luang. It's a charming place to wander around, set in a sizeable compound with huge trees at the boundaries. Judging by the remains, it must have once been an impressive monument. Only the Buddha in the northern niche is original; the others are reproductions. To the west of the *chedi* is a reclining Buddha in an open pavilion.

Chiang Mai's rather dull city pillar is found in a small shrine close to the large *viharn*, at the western side of the monastery compound. This is the foundation stone of the city and home to Chiang Mai's guardian spirits. These must be periodically appeased if the city is to prosper.

Wat Duang Dii

Just north of the intersection of Rachdamnern and Phra Pokklao roads, is peaceful Wat Duang Dii. The compound contains three northern Thai wooden temple buildings, with fine woodcarving and attractively weathered doors; note the small, almost Chinese, pagoda-roofed structure to the left of the gate with its meticulous stucco work. Behind the *viharn* and *bot* is a *chedi* with elephants at each corner, topped with copper plate.

Wat Suan Dok

Outside the walls, Wat Suan Dok lies to the west of town on Suthep Road (Chiang Mai map, page 22). Originally built in 1371 but subsequently restored and enlarged, the wat contains the ashes of Chiang Mai's royal family, housed in white, variously shaped, mini-*chedis*. Much of the monastery was erected during the reign of King Kawila (1782-1813). The large central *chedi* is said to house eight relics of the Lord Buddha.

The *bot* is usually open to the public and has a large, brightly lit, gilded bronze Buddha image in the Chiang Saen style. The walls are decorated with lively, rather gaudy, scenes from the Jataka stories. Above the entrance is a mural showing the Buddha's mother being impregnated by a white elephant (highly auspicious), while on the left-hand wall is depicted (along with several other episodes from the Buddha's life) the moment when, as a prince (note the fine clothes and jewellery), he renounces his wealth and position and symbolically cuts his hair.

Wat Umong

ⓘ *Take a songthaew along Suthep Rd and ask to be let off at the turning for Wat Umong. It is about a 1-km walk from here (turn left almost opposite the gates to Chiang Mai University, just past a market travelling west).*

The wat was founded in 1371 by King Ku Na (1355-1385) who promoted the establishment of a new, ascetic school of forest-dwelling monks. In 1369 he brought a leading Sukhothai monk to Chiang Mai – the Venerable Sumana – and built Wat Umong for him and his followers. Sumana studied here until his death in 1389. Although the wat is at the edge

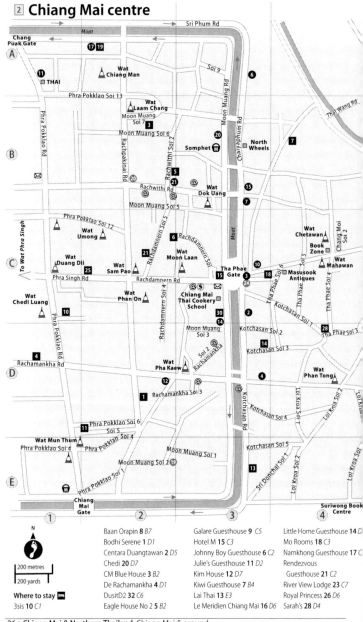

② Chiang Mai centre

Where to stay

3sis **10** *C1*

Baan Orapin **8** *B7*
Bodhi Serene **1** *D1*
Centara Duangtawan **2** *D5*
Chedi **20** *D7*
CM Blue House **3** *B2*
De Rachamankha **4** *D1*
DusitD2 **32** *C6*
Eagle House No 2 **5** *B2*

Galare Guesthouse **9** *C5*
Hotel M **15** *C3*
Johnny Boy Guesthouse **6** *C2*
Julie's Guesthouse **11** *D2*
Kim House **12** *D7*
Kiwi Guesthouse **7** *B4*
Lai Thai **13** *E3*
Le Meridien Chiang Mai **16** *D6*

Little Home Guesthouse **14** *D*
Mo Rooms **18** *C3*
Namkhong Guesthouse **17** *C*
Rendezvous
  Guesthouse **21** *C2*
River View Lodge **23** *C7*
Royal Princess **26** *D6*
Sarah's **28** *D4*

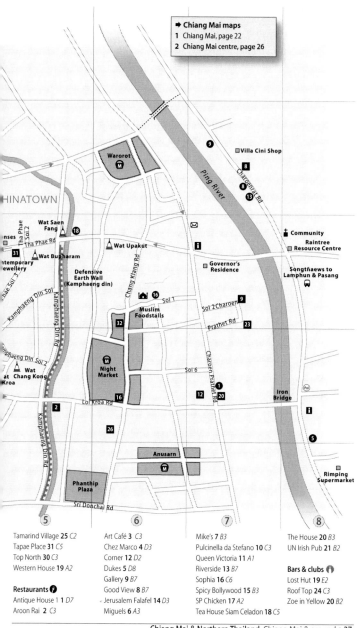

→ **Chiang Mai maps**
1 Chiang Mai, page 22
2 Chiang Mai centre, page 26

CHINATOWN

Villa Cini Shop

Wat Saen Fang

Wat Bupharam

Wat Upakut

Governor's Residence

Community

Raintree Resource Centre

Songthaews to Lamphun & Pasang

Defensive Earth Wall (Kamphaeng din)

Muslim Foodstalls

Night Market

Wat Chang Kong Kroa

Iron Bridge

Anusarn

Phanthip Plaza

Rimping Supermarket

Sri Donchai Rd

Tamarind Village **25** *C2*
Tapae Place **31** *C5*
Top North **30** *C3*
Western House **19** *A2*

Restaurants 🍴
Antique House 1 **1** *D7*
Aroon Rai **2** *C3*

Art Café **3** *C3*
Chez Marco **4** *D3*
Corner **12** *D2*
Dukes **5** *D8*
Gallery **9** *B7*
Good View **8** *B7*
Jerusalem Falafel **14** *D3*
Miguels **6** *A3*

Mike's **7** *B3*
Pulcinella da Stefano **10** *C3*
Queen Victoria **11** *A1*
Riverside **13** *B7*
Sophia **16** *C6*
Spicy Bollywood **15** *B3*
SP Chicken **17** *A2*
Tea House Siam Celadon **18** *C5*

The House **20** *B3*
UN Irish Pub **21** *B2*

Bars & clubs 🍸
Lost Hut **19** *E2*
Roof Top **24** *C3*
Zoe in Yellow **20** *B2*

of the city, set in areas of woodland, it feels much more distant. There are tunnels which house several Buddha images. The wat was abandoned in the 19th century and the *chedi* pillaged for its treasures some years later. It became a functioning wat again in 1948. From the trees hang Thai proverbs and sayings from the Buddhist texts, extolling pilgrims to lead good and productive lives.

Chiang Mai University Art Center

ⓘ *239 Nimmanhaemin Rd, corner of Nimmanhaemin and Suthep roads, T053-944833, www.cmumuseum.org. Tue-Sun 0900-1700.*

The large, modern Chiang Mai University Art Center (see map, page 22) displays modern fine art, including paintings, sculpture, installation works and prints by mostly Thai artists. There are occasional temporary exhibitions of work by non-Thais. Other activities include concerts and puppet shows. It is interesting for displaying the progress of Thai fine art, but hardly world class. The small but chic **Art Café** and the shop (selling books and ceramics) are classier than the works displayed.

Wat Jet Yod

The beautiful Wat Jet Yod (literally, 'seven spires') is just off the Superhighway at the intersection with Ladda Land Rd, northwest of the city and close to the National Museum (see map, page 22). It was founded in 1453 and contains a highly unusual square *chedi* with seven spires. These represent the seven weeks the Buddha resided in the gardens at Bodhgaya, after his enlightenment under the Bodhi tree. According to the chronicles the structure is a copy of the 13th-century Mahabodhi temple in Pagan, Burma, which itself was a copy of the famous temple at Bodhgaya in Bihar (although it is hard to see the resemblance). On the faces of the *chedi* are an assortment of superbly modelled stucco figures in bas-relief, while at one end is a niche containing a large Buddha image – dating from 1455 – in an attitude of subduing Mara (now protected behind steel bars). The stucco work represents the 70 celestial deities and are among the finest works from the Lanna School of Art.

National Museum

ⓘ *T053-221308, www.thailandmuseum.com, Wed-Sun 0900-1600. ฿30100. Take bus No 6.*

The National Museum (see map, page 22) lies just to the east of Wat Jet Yod on Highway 11 and has a fine collection of Buddha images and Sawankhalok china downstairs, as well as some impressive ethnological exhibits upstairs.

Other wats

Wat Ku Tao (see map, page 22), to the north of the city off Chotana Road, dates from 1613. It is situated in a leafy compound and has an unusual *chedi*, shaped like a pile of inverted alms bowls. Others worth a fleeting visit for those not yet 'watted out' include: **Wat Chetawan**, **Wat Mahawan**, **Wat Saen Fang** and **Wat Bupharam** – all on Tha Phae Road (see map, page 26) – between the east walls of the city and the Ping River. Wat Mahawan displays some accomplished woodcarving on its *viharn*, washed in a delicate yellow, while the stupa is guarded by an array of *singhas* (mythical lions) – some with bodies hanging from their gaping jaws. Wat Bupharam has two old *viharns* a small *bot* and a stupa.

Markets and Chinatown

The night market dominates the west side of Chang Klang Road (see map, page 22). It comprises a number of purpose-built buildings with hundreds of stalls, selling a huge array of tribal goods as well as clothing, jewellery and other tourist goodies (see Shopping, page 49). For a completely different atmosphere, walk through Chiang Mai's Chinatown which lies to the north of Tha Phae Road, between the moat and the river. Small workshops run by entrepreneurial Sino-Thais jostle between excellent small restaurants serving reasonably priced Thai and Chinese food. Near the river, and running two or three streets in from the river, is the **Warorot Market** (see map, page 27), the city's largest. It starts on Praisani Road, close to the river, as a flower market, but transforms into a mixed market with fruit, vegetables, dried fish, pigs' heads and trotters, great dollops of buffalo flesh, crabs, dried beans and deep-fried pork skin. There are several large covered market areas with clothes, textiles, shoes, leather goods, Chinese funeral accessories, stationery and baskets.

Museum of World Insects and Natural Wonders

ⓘ *72 Nimmanhaemin Soi 13, T053-211891, www.insectmuseumthailand.multiply.com. Open 0900-1700. ฿300, ฿100 children.*

Manop and Rampa Rattanarithikul are a likeable and very knowledgeable couple who take pleasure in showing you around their home, which since 1999, has become a mausoleum for thousands of insectoid beasties (see map, page 22). Rampa's specialism is mosquitoes; there are 420 species of mosquito in Thailand, 18 of which she personally identified and categorized, travelling to London to check the type specimens in the Natural History Museum. There are interesting collections of shells, fossils, petrified wood and, of course, case after case of bugs, including beetles, moths, roaches and butterflies. The same family owns a smaller insect museum on Rachdamern Road in the Old City. Recommended.

Around Chiang Mai → *For listings, see pages 38-60.*

Doi Suthep

ⓘ *Take a songthaew from town to the zoo (฿20) and switch to a shared songthaew there (฿40). A taxi should cost about ฿300 return. The temple is closed after 1630 and charges a ฿20 entry fee to foreigners only.*

Overlooking Chiang Mai, 16 km to the northwest, is Doi Suthep (Suthep Mountain) a very popular pilgrimage spot for Thais, perched on the hillside and offering spectacular views of the city and plain below. A steep, winding road climbs 1000 m to the base of a 300-step *naga* staircase, which in turn leads up to **Wat Phrathat**. Initially, you'd be forgiven for thinking you'd arrived at a tacky theme park rather than a revered site, such is the proliferation of overpriced souvenir stalls. And, where foreign tourists are concerned, everybody seems to be on the make, from the tuk-tuk drivers through to the surly temple staff who make sure no foreigner enters without their ฿30 ticket. Some Thais have complained that Doi Suthep is becoming degraded by the influence of tourism, yet the same critics have failed to address the fact that the temple guardians themselves have adopted commercial practices.

If you don't fancy the climb take the cable car (฿20). A white elephant is alleged to have collapsed here, after King Ku Na (1355-1385) gave it the task of finding an auspicious site for a shrine to house a holy relic of the Lord Buddha.

The 24-m-high *chedi* has a number of Buddha images in both Sukhothai and Chiang Saen styles, arrayed in the gallery surrounding it. The whole compound is surrounded by bells (which visitors can no longer ring). If you're brave enough, this trip is best done by motorbike, which will allow you to take in the waterfalls and viewing points en route. The road is bendy but in good condition, and it's a beautiful drive.

Hilltribes

A visit to a hilltribe village is one of the main reasons why people travel to the north of Thailand. The hilltribe population (*Chao Khao* – 'Mountain People' – in Thai) numbers about 800,000, or a little over 1% of the total population of the country.

These 800,000 people are far from homogenous: each hilltribe (there are nine recognized by the government), has a different language, dress, religion, artistic heritage and culture. They meet their subsistence needs in different ways and often occupy different ecological niches. In some respects they are as far removed from one another as they are from the low-land Thais.

As their name suggests, the hilltribes occupy the highland areas that fringe the northern region, with the largest populations in the provinces of Chiang Mai (143,000), Chiang Rai (98,000), Mae Hong Son (83,000) and Tak (69,000). These figures are a few years old, but the relative balance between the provinces has not changed significantly. Although this guide follows the tradition of using the term 'hilltribe' to describe these diverse peoples, it is in many regards an unfortunate one. They are not tribes in the anthropological sense, derived as it is from the study of the peoples of Africa. For information on trekking and choosing a trek operator, see box, page 56.

Etiquette and customs vary between the hilltribes. However, the following are general rules of good behaviour that should be adhered to whenever possible.
→ Dress modestly and avoid undressing/changing in public.
→ Ask permission before photographing anyone (old people and pregnant women often object to having their photograph taken). Be aware that hill people are unlikely to pose out of the kindness of their hearts – don't begrudge them the money; for many, tourism is their livelihood.
→ Ask permission before entering a house.
→ Do not touch or photograph village shrines.
→ Do not smoke opium.
→ Avoid sitting or stepping on door sills.
→ Avoid excessive displays of wealth and be sensitive when giving gifts (for children, pens are better than sweets).
→ Avoid introducing Western medicines.

Phu Ping Palace
① *Fri-Sun and public holidays 0830-1630 when the royal family is not in residence. Songthaews from Doi Suthep to Phu Ping, ฿50.*
The winter residence of the King, Phu Ping Palace, is 5 km past Wat Phrathat. The immaculate gardens are open to the public when the family is not in residence.

Doi Pui
① *Charter a songthaew; alternatively take a songthaew from the zoo, Doi Suthep or Phu Ping Palace.*
Rather commercialized, Meo village, 4 km past Phu Ping Palace, is only worth a visit for those unable to get to other villages. There are two second-rate museum huts, one focusing on opium production, the other on the different hilltribes. On the hillside above the village is an English flower garden, which is in full bloom in January.

Tribal Museum

ⓘ *T053-210872, Mon-Fri 0900-1600. Take a songthaew from the city (₱50). It takes about 15-20 mins to walk to the museum.*

The Tribal Museum, attached to the **Tribal Research Institute**, overlooks a lake in Rachamankha Park, 5 km north of town off Chotana Road. The building itself looks like a cross between a rocket and a *chedi* and it houses the fine collection of tribal pieces that were formerly held at Chiang Mai University's Tribal Research Centre. Carefully and professionally presented, the pieces on show include textiles, agricultural implements, musical instruments, jewellery and weapons. The museum is particularly worth visiting for those intending to go trekking (see box, page 56).

Wiang Kum Kam

ⓘ *Accessible by bicycle, motorbike or tuk-tuk. Take Route 106 south towards Lamphun; the ruins are signposted off to the right about 5 km from Chiang Mai – but only in Thai – from where it is another 2 km. Look out for a ruined chedi on the right and ask along the way for confirmation. To get to Wat Kan Thom, take the yellow sign to the left about 800 m from the main road. It's about a 10- to 15-min walk from the main road. For Wat Chedi Liam, follow the land all the way to the river road (Koh Klang Rd), about 2 km or so, and turn left. The Wat is about 200 m down here, on the left – impossible to miss.*

Wiang Kum Kam is a ruined city, 5 km south of Chiang Mai, which was established by the Mon in the 12th or 13th centuries and abandoned in the 18th century. The gardens and ruins are beautiful and peaceful, dotted with bodhi trees. Today, archaeologists are beginning to uncover a site of about 9 sq km which contains the remains of at least 20 wats. It was discovered in 1984 when rumours surfaced that a hoard of valuable amulets were found. Treasure seekers began to dig up the grounds of the Wat Chang Kham monastery until the Fine Arts Department intervened and began a systematic survey of the site to reveal Wiang Kum Kam. The most complete monument is Wat Chang Kham, which has a marvellous bronze *naga* outside. In front of the wat is the spirit chamber of Chiang Mai's founder, King Mengrai. Nearby are the ruins of Wat Noi and two dilapidated *chedis*. Perhaps the most impressive single structure is the renovated *chedi* at Wat Chedi Liam. This takes the form of a stepped pyramid – a unique Mon architectural style of which there are only a handful of examples in Thailand.

Bor Sang and San Kamphaeng circuit

A pleasant 75-km day trip takes you east of the city, visiting craft centres a couple of interesting wats, some incredible caves and a hot spring. Almost immediately after leaving the city along Route 1006 (Charoen Muang Road), kilns, paper factories and lacquerware stalls start to appear, and continue for a full 15 km all the way to Bor Sang.

Bor Sang is famous for its handmade, painted paper umbrellas. The shaft is crafted from local softwood, the ribs from bamboo, and the covering from oiled rice paper. The **Umbrella Festival** in January is a colourful affair. Beyond Bor Sang is San Kamphaeng, another craft village, which has expanded and diversified so that it has effectively merged with Bor Sang – at least in terms of shopping. If you make it as far as San Kamphaeng, there is a good Muslim restaurant at the intersection with the main road (left hand, near side) serving chicken biryani, other Indian dishes, ice creams and cappuccino.

For **Wat Pa Tung**, which is 10 km on from San Kamphaeng, take a right-hand fork onto Route 1147. At the junction with Route 1317, cross over the road (signposted towards the Chiang Mai-Lamphun Golf Club). Where the road takes a sharp right (with another signpost for the golf club), continue straight ahead on the minor road. About 3 km on is Wat Pa Tung. This wat is a lively and popular modern wat, set amongst sugar palms and rice fields. Its popularity rests on the fact that the revered Luang Phu La Chaiya Janto (an influential thinker and preacher and highly regarded for his asceticism) lived here to the ripe old age of 96. When he died in 1993 his rather diminutive body was entombed in a sealed glass coffin, which was then placed in a specially built stilted modern *kuti* where it still resides today.

From Wat Pa Tung, return to Route 1317 and turn right. After about 10 km, on the left, you will see a rocky outcrop with flags fluttering from the top; this is the only marker for the **Muang On Caves** ① *open daily during daylight hours, ฿20*; take a left turning (no sign in English) and wind up a lane, past a forest of ordained trees, to the car park. From here there are around 170 steps up a *naga* staircase to the entrance to the caves, with great views over the valley. The entrance to the caves is tricky and the steps very steep, with low overhangs of rock. But it is worth the sweating and bending; the cave opens up into a series of impressive caverns with a large stalagmite wrapped with sacred cloth and a number of images of the Buddha. There are drink stalls at the car park.

At the foot of the hill (before returning to the main road), take a left turn for the back route (2.5 km) to the **Roong Arun Hot Springs** ① *฿30, ฿15 children, public baths ฿60*. Here, sulphur springs bubble up into an artificial pond, where visitors can buy chicken or quail eggs to boil in wicker baskets hung from bamboo rods. The springs reach boiling point; if you want a dip head for the public baths, where the water is cooled. A full range of massages, mud baths, saunas and herbal treatments are also available. Return to Chiang Mai by way of Route 118 – about a 20-minute drive.

Mae Sa Valley – Samoeng circuit
① *Buses and songthaews run along this route, but it would be much more convenient to do the round-trip by hire car or motorbike.*
The 100-km loop from Chiang Mai along the Mae Sa Valley to Samoeng and then back along Route 1269 is an attractive drive that can easily be accomplished in a day. Travel north on Route 107 out of town and then turn west onto Route 1096, in the district town of Mae Rim. From here the road follows the course of the Mae Sa River. Just past Mae Rim are a couple of exclusive shops selling 'antiques'. At the Km 5 marker is the sign for the **Tad Mok Waterfalls**, which lie 9 km off the main road to the right. These are less popular than the Mae Sa Falls a couple of kilometres on from here (see below), but still worthwhile.

Continuing west on the main road, there are two more orchid gardens: **Suan Bua Mae Sa Orchid** ① *between the Km 5 and Km 6 markers, 0800-1600*, and **Mae Rim Orchid and Butterfly Farm** ① *at the Km 6 marker, 0800-1600, ฿20*. The orchids are beautiful, the butterflies even more so (watch them emerge from their chrysalises), but the food is average and overpriced.

Mae Sa Waterfall ① *0800-1800, ฿10, ฿30 per car*, is located in the **Doi Suthep-Pui National Park**, 1 km off Route 1096 (to the left) and about 1 km beyond the orchid farm. The waterfall is in fact a succession of mini-falls – relatively peaceful, with a visitor centre and a number of stalls.

But the most popular destination of all in the valley, 3 km further on from the waterfall, is the **Elephant Training Camp** ① *T053-206247, www.maesaelephantcamp.com, 3 shows daily 0800, 0940 and 1330, ฿200, elephant riding ฿800-1200 for 2 people. Mahout training courses also available.* Elephants are well cared for here (with a number of babies, which must be a good indicator of their happiness). Visitors can see the elephants bathing, feed them bananas and sugarcane and then watch an elephant show.

Queen Sirikit Botanical Gardens ① *T053-841333, www.qsbg.org, 0830-1630, ฿100, ฿50 child, ฿100 car*, was established in 1993 on the edge of the Doi Suthep-Pui National Park, 12 km from the Mae Rim turn-off. The great bulk of the gardens was designated a conservation area before 1993, and there are a number of large trees. It is Thailand's first botanical gardens and a truly impressive enterprise. There are three marked trails (rock garden and nursery plus waterfall, arboreta and climber trail), a museum and an information centre. But the highlight of the gardens is the glasshouse complex. The largest features a waterfall and elevated boardwalk, and there are also glasshouses for desert flora, savannah flora and wetland plants.

Mae Sa Craft Village ① *T053-290052*, is a leafy resort spread over a hillside, with immaculately kept gardens of brightly coloured annual flowers. There are dozens of great activities to get involved in. *➤➤ See Where to stay, page 42, and Tour operators, page 55.*

Continuing further on along Route 1096 there are, in turn, the **Mae Yim Falls** (17 km), **Doi Sang** – a Meo village (25 km) – and the **Nang Koi Falls** (34 km). At the furthest point in this loop is **Samoeng**, the district capital. There's little to do here unless you arrive for Samoeng's annual **strawberry festival** held in January or February.

Continuing on from Samoeng, the road skirts around the heavily forested **Doi Suthep-Pui National Park**. The winding road finally descends from the hills and comes out by the north-south irrigation canal at the village of Ban Ton Khwen. Just before you reach the canal is a turning to the right and, a little further along, the bare brick walls of **Wat Inthrawat**. The entrance at the back is by a cluster of sugar palms. This spectacular *viharn* was built in 1858 in Lanna style. Its graceful roofs and detailed woodcarving are a fine sight. Return to Chiang Mai by way of the canal road (turn left at the junction) or on Route 108 (the Hang Dong road), which is a little further to the east of the canal road.

Chiang Dao Elephant Training Centre

① *56 km from Chiang Mai on the route north to Fang, about 15 km south of Chiang Dao, T081-0275009, www.chiangdaoelephantcamp.com. ฿60. Numerous companies offer tours to the centre from Chiang Mai, but it is easy enough to get here by public transport as it is on the main road.*

This elephant training centre at Chiang Dao offers shows (฿100), elephant riding (฿800-1400) and rafting (฿400). There is a second elephant camp, 17 km south of Chiang Dao, the **Mae Ping Elephant Camp**, which is not as good.

Chiang Dao

① *As Chiang Dao is on the main Chiang Mai–Fang road, there are numerous buses and songthaews from the Chang Puak bus station.*

Chiang Dao, a district town 70 km north of Chiang Mai, is a useful stopping-off point for visitors to the Chiang Dao Caves (see below). The surfaced road running east from the town leads to a series of hilltribe villages: Palong, Mussur, Lahu and Karen. Most of these are situated on public forest reserve land and many of the inhabitants do not have Thai citizenship. They have built simple huts where tourists can stay, and a number of trekking companies in Chiang Mai begin or end their treks in the villages here. The town has a number of good restaurants; of particular note is the locally renowned **Bun Thong Phanit** (on the left-hand side, travelling north, in a wooden shophouse), which serves excellent *khao kha muu* (boiled pork leg with rice).

Chiang Dao Caves

ⓘ ฿20 to go as far as the electric light system extends; ฿100 to hire a guide with lamp for a 40-min tour deeper into the caves (guides congregate 100 m or so into the caves where a rota system ensures an equal share of business). Catch a bus to Fang from the Chang Puak bus station on Chotana Rd and get off at Chiang Dao. Songthaews take visitors the final 6 km from the main road to the caves. A songthaew directly to the caves and back should cost about ฿1000 each way (1½ hrs). It is also possible to hire motorbikes and bicycles in Chiang Dao itself – from the 'tourist corner' on the left-hand side of the main road, shortly before reaching the turn-off for the caves (turn left in the town of Chiang Dao, just after the Km 72 marker; it is clearly signposted).

These caves, 78 km north of Chiang Mai on Route 107, penetrate deep into the limestone hills and are associated with Wat Chiang Dao. They are among the most extensive in Thailand and are a popular pilgrimage spot for monks and ordinary Thais. There is a profusion of stalls here, many selling herbal remedies said to cure most ailments. The caverns contain Buddha and hermit images, as well as impressive natural rock formations. Electric lights have been installed, but only as far as the **Tham Phra Non** (Cave of the Reclining Buddha), where a royal coat of arms on the cave wall records Queen Sirikit's visit to the caves. To explore further it is necessary to hire a guide.

Lamphun

ⓘ Most people visit Lamphun from Chiang Mai and regular (blue) songthaews run along the old Lamphun–Chiang Mai Rd, leaving Chiang Mai just over the Nawarat Bridge, near the TAT office (30-40 mins, ฿15). They can be picked up by the National Museum too. The train station is 2 km north off Charoenrat Rd, 5 daily connections with Bangkok and Chiang Mai. If travelling to Lamphun from Chiang Mai it is worth taking the old road, which, for a 10-km stretch, is lined with an avenue of Yang trees. Only the action of activist monks, who ordained the trees, saved them from felling.

This quiet, historic city lies 26 km south of Chiang Mai, and is famous for its *longans* (small tropical fruit) – there's a **Longan Fair** every August with a contest to judge both the best fruit and to select the year's Miss Lamyai (*longan*). It is also a venerated place of Buddhist teaching at **Wat Phra That Haripunjaya**. This famous temple has a 50-m-tall *chedi* crowned by a solid gold nine-tiered honorific umbrella (weighing, apparently, 6498.75 g). Another renowned temple is **Wat Chama Devi**, which lies 1 km west of the moat on Chama Devi Road. It is said that Princess Chama Devi selected the spot by having an archer shoot an arrow to the north from town – her ashes are contained within the main *chedi*. Built in 1218, this square-based *chedi* of brick and stucco has five tiers of niches, each containing a beautiful standing Buddha.

Lamphun, which was founded in AD 600, is sited on the banks of the Ping River and was formerly the capital of the Haripunjaya Kingdom. The moat and parts of the old defensive walls are still present and it was a powerful centre of the Mon culture until King Mengrai succeeded in taking the city in 1281.

Lampang → Phone code: 054.

ⓘ Regular buses from Nawarat Bridge or from the Arcade terminal and trains connect with Chiang Mai (2 hrs) while local transport is provided by the town's horse-drawn carriages and songthaews.

An atmospheric provincial capital complete with horse-drawn carriages, soothing riverside hang-outs and the sumptuous temple of Wat Phra That Lampang Luang, Lampang makes a great day or overnight trip from Chiang Mai. A tour around town in a horse-drawn carriage costs ฿200-300. They generally take two routes, the cheaper one takes about 30 minutes, the more expensive one an hour or alternatively ฿300 per hour. There's some decent accommodation and a chance to indulge in a leisurely lunch at one of the great riverside restaurants. The airport is on the south edge of town, off Prabhat Road, and the bus station is on Route 1, just east of the railway line (a 15-minute walk to the town centre). The railway station is on the west side of town, at the end of Surain Road. *Songthaews* run routes around town (although these are flexibly interpreted); the *rop muang* or *rop wiang* ('around town') are the most useful (฿15 anywhere in town).

Established in the seventh-century Dvaravati period, Lampang prospered as a trading centre, with a wealth of ornate and well-endowed wats. Re-built in the 19th century as a fortified *wiang* (a walled city), it became an important centre for the teak industry with British loggers making this one of their key centres. The influence of the Burmese is reflected in the architecture of some of the more important wats – a number still have Burmese abbots.

Wat Phra Kaeo Don Tao ⓘ ฿20, and its 'sister' **Wat Chadaram** are to be found on Phra Kaeo Road, north across the Rachada Phisek Bridge. Wat Phra Kaeo housed the renowned Emerald Buddha (the Phra Kaeo – now in Wat Phra Kaeo, Bangkok) for 32 years during the 15th century. This royal temple is said to be imbued with particular spiritual power and significance, largely because of its association with the Phra Kaeo. The ceilings and columns of the 18th-century *viharn* are carved in wood and are intricately inlaid with porcelain and enamel. In the compound, there is also a Burmese-style chapel (probably late 18th century) and a golden *chedi*. Next door, Wat Chadaram contains the most attractive building in the whole complex: a small, intimate, well-proportioned, wooden *viharn*.

Wat Chedi Sao ⓘ 0800-1700, the 'temple of the 20 chedis', is 3 km northeast of the town, 1 km off the Lampang–Jae Hom road at Ban Wang Moh. A large white *chedi* is surrounded by 19 smaller ones, and a strange assortment of concrete animals and monks. The most important Buddha image here is a gold, seated image cast in the 15th century. Its importance stems both from its miraculous discovery – by a local farmer in his rice field in 1983 – and from the fact that it is said to contain a piece of the Lord Buddha's skull in its head. To reach the wat, walk over the bridge to the junction of Jhamatawee and Wangkhon roads and hail a *saamlor* there for ฿5.

Wat Sri Chum ⓘ Tippowan Rd (aka Sri Chum Rd), 0700-1830, ฿20, is a beautiful wat, constructed 200 years ago and regarded as one of the finest Burmese-style wats in Thailand. Tragically, the richly carved and painted *viharn*, was destroyed by fire in 1993. The compound exudes an ambience of peaceful meditation, although it is in urgent need of funds to complete restoration.

Wat Phra That Lampang Luang

ⓘ 0900-1200, 1300-1700, donation; there are drinks and foodstalls in the car park area across the road from the wat. Take a songthaew to Ko Kha and then a motorbike taxi the last 2.5 km to the wat. Songthaews for Ko Kha run regularly along Phahonyothin Rd. Alternatively, charter a songthaew from Lampang (฿300-400). If travelling by private transport from Lampang, drive along Route 1 towards Ko Kha. In Ko Kha pass through the town, over the bridge, and then turn right at the T-junction onto Route 1034. The wat is 2.5 km away – just off Route 1034 (the chedi can be seen rising up behind some sugar palms). From Chiang Mai, turn right off Route 11 just past the Km 80 marker, signposted to Ko Kha.

The monastery stands on a slight hill, surrounded by a brick wall – all that remains of the original fortressed city which was sited here more than 1000 years ago. Sand and tiles, rather than concrete, surround the monuments. While the buildings have been restored on a number of occasions over the years, it remains beautifully complete and authentic.

Originally this wat was a fortified site, protected by walls, moats and ramparts. Approached by a staircase flanked by guardian lions and *nagas*, visitors enter through an archway of intricate 15th-century stone carving. The large, open central *viharn*, **Viharn Luang**, houses a *ku* – a brick, stucco and gilded pyramid peculiar to northern wats – containing a Buddha image (dating from 1563), a collection of thrones and some wall paintings. The building, with its intricate woodcarving and fine pattern work on the pillars and ceiling, is dazzling.

Behind the *viharn* is the principal **chedi**, 45 m high it contains three relics of the Buddha: a hair and the ashes of the Buddha's right forehead and neck bone. Made of beaten copper and brass plates over a brick core, it is typically Lanna Thai in style and was erected in the late 15th century. The **Buddha Viharn** to the left of the *chedi* is thought to date from the 13th century and was restored in 1802. Beautifully carved and painted, it contains a seated Buddha image. Immediately behind this *viharn* is a small, raised building housing a **footprint of the Buddha** (only men are permitted). This building houses a camera obscura; at certain times of day (from late morning through to early afternoon) the sun's rays pass through a small hole in the building's wall, projecting an inverted image of the *chedi* and the surrounding buildings onto a sheet.

To the right of the main *viharn* are two more small, but equally beautiful, *viharns*: the **Viharn Nam Taem** and the **Viharn Ton Kaew**. The former is thought to date from the early 16th century, and may be the oldest wooden building in Thailand. It also contains some old wall paintings, although these are difficult to see in the gloom. Finally within the walls are the **Viharn Phra Chao Sila**, built to enshrine a stone image of the Buddha.

Outside the walls, through the southern doorway, is an enormous and ancient **bodhi tree**, supported by a veritable army of crutches. Close by is a small, musty and rather unexciting **museum**. Next to this is a fine raised scripture library and a *viharn*, within which is another revered **Emerald Buddha** – heavily obscured by two rows of steel bars. It is rumoured to have been made from the same block of jasper as the famous Emerald Buddha in Bangkok.

Thai Elephant Conservation Centre

① *T054-829333, www.thailandelephant.org. Bathing sessions daily at 0945, shows daily at 1000, 1100 and 1330, ฿170. Elephant rides ฿500 for 30 mins, ฿1000 for 1 hr. There is also a small restaurant, souvenir shop and toilets. The ECC also runs English-language mahout training courses – contact them directly for details. Take an early morning bus towards Chiang Mai; the elephant centre is about 30 km before Lampang, just before the driver where you're going. From the road it is a 1.8-km walk by road or take a short cut through the forest. Alternatively charter a songthaew from town for about ฿600 return. It is possible to stay at the camp; see the website for further details.*

The recent fate of the Thai elephant has been a slow inexorable decline. Numbers are dwindling and the few that do remain are mainly used as tourist attractions (see page 32). Many of the places that offer chances to interact with elephants are poorly run, treating their charges with contempt. Not so the excellent Thai Elephant Conservation Centre, northwest of Lampang near Thung Kwian, on the road to Chiang Mai (Highway 11). Here elephants are trained for forest work, others are released back into the wild; there are elephant musicians, elephant artists and elephant dung paper. There's even an elephant hospital and rescue centre. All in all there are about 50 animals here.

Pha Thai caves

ⓘ *The first 400 m of the cave is open to the public but the great majority of the system is off-limits. Refreshments are available. Take Route 1 from Lampang towards Ngao and 19 km before Ngao turn left for the caves.*

The Pha Thai caves are some of the most spectacular in Thailand; the cave system is one of the country's deepest too, extending more than 1200 m. The caves are renowned not only for their length but also for the quantity of snakes that have taken up residence here. From the arrival point to the cave entrance visitors have to climb 283 steps. As with many caves, it has acquired religious significance and the cave is associated with a wat. A white *chedi* stands like a sentinel just outside the mouth of the cave and a large gilded Buddha fills the entrance itself.

Jai Sorn (Chae Sorn) National Park

ⓘ *Take the road from Lampang towards Wak Nua and then turn left at the Km 58-59 marker. Continue along this road for another 17 km.*

The park, Lampang's only protected area, has hot volcanic springs in the waterfall pools – the Chae Son Waterfall and Chae Son Hot Spa Park, which are just 1 km apart. The waterfall tumbles down seven levels and during the wet season is particularly spectacular. The hot springs bubble out at 75-80°C, are mixed with cold water from the waterfall and are channelled into 11 bathrooms.

Doi Inthanon National Park

ⓘ *0600-1800, ฿400, ฿200 children. ฿50 car, ฿20 motorbike, ฿50 songthaew and minibus. Best time to visit: just after the end of the rainy season, in late Oct or Nov. By Jan and Feb the air becomes hazy, not least because of forest fires. Buses, minibuses and songthaews for Hang Dong and Chom Thong leave from the Chiang Mai Gate. Take a yellow songthaew for the 58 km from Chiang Mai Gate to Chom Thong (฿15). From Chom Thong market, take another yellow songthaew to the Mae Klang Falls (฿10) or the Wachiratan Falls (฿15). To reach Mae Ya Falls and Doi Inthanon summit, a songthaew must be chartered (this will seat 10 people); ฿500 and ฿700 respectively. From Hang Dong there are songthaews to Doi Inthanon.*

Located off Route 108, on Route 1009, Doi Inthanon is Thailand's highest peak at 2595 m. The mountain is a national park and the winding route to the top is stunning, with terraced rice fields, cultivated valleys and a few hilltribe villages. The park covers 482 sq km and is one of the most visited in Thailand. Although the drive to the top is dramatic, the park's flora and fauna can only really be appreciated by taking one of the hiking trails off the main road. The flora ranges from dry deciduous forest on the lower slopes, to moist evergreen between 1000 m and 1800 m, and 'cloud' forest and a sphagnum (moss) bog towards the summit. There are even some relict pines. Once the habitat of bears and tigers, the wildlife has been severely depleted through over-hunting. However, it is still possible to see flying squirrel, red-toothed shrew, Chinese pangolin and Pere David's vole, as well as an abundance of butterflies and moths. Although the mountain, in its entirety, is a national park, there are several thousand Hmong and Karen living here and cultivating the slopes.

Just beneath the summit, in a spectacular position, are a pair of bronze and gold-tiled *chedis*, one dedicated to the king in 1989 and the other dedicated to Queen Sirikit at the end of 1992. Both *chedis* contain intricate symbolism and have been built to reaffirm the unity of the Thai nation. The ashes of Chiang Mai's last king, Inthawichayanon, are contained in a small white *chedi* on the summit – the ultimate reflection of the idea that no one should be higher than the king, in life or in death.

There are a number of waterfalls on the slopes: the **Mae Klang Falls** (near the Km 8 marker and not far from the visitor centre), **Wachiratan Falls** (26 km down from the summit and near the Km 21 marker, restaurant here) and **Siriphum Falls** (3-4 km off the road near the Km 31 marker and not far from the park headquarters), as well as the large **Borichinda Cave** (a 2-km hike off the main road near the visitor centre at the Km 9 marker). Note that it is a tiring climb up steep steps to the Mae Klang and Wachiratan falls. The **Mae Ya Falls** in the south of the park are the most spectacular, plunging more than 250 m (they lie 15 km from park headquarters and are accessible from Chom Thong town). Ask for details at the visitor centre a few kilometres on from the park's entrance.

Chiang Mai and around listings

For hotel and restaurant price codes and other relevant information, see pages 8-12.

😑 Where to stay

Chiang Mai *p20, maps p22 and p26*
Chiang Mai has a huge range of places to stay, mostly concentrated to the east of the old walled city, although there is a significant group of guesthouses to be found west of Moon Muang Rd, south of Tha Phae Gate. Many of the mid-range and high-end hotels are located in the night market area. It is rare for visitors to have to pay the set room (rack) rate.

Old City
Within the old city walls and the moat is the greatest concentration of guesthouses, as well as a growing selection of mid-range and more expensive options. Most are to be found in the eastern half. The old city is relatively quiet and tree-filled and away from the main centre of commercial activity. It is about a 15-min walk to the night market, although there are plenty of bars, restaurants, tour operators, laundries and motorbike and car rental outfits nearby.

$$$$ Bodhi Serene, 110 Ratchaphakhinai Rd, T053-903900, www.boutique-hotel-chiangmai.com. Sleek boutique hotel in a pleasant part of the old city. Wooden floors, balconies and giant flat-screen TVs all trimmed with the usual contemporary Thai details.

$$$$ Rachamankha, 6 Rachamanka 9, Phra Singh Rd, T053-904 111, www.rachamankha.com. This oasis of almost meditative calm is a stunning medium-sized boutique hotel modelled on Lanna temple architecture and with a designer's eye for detail, all built using traditional techniques. The a/c rooms can be a bit small and dark but are filled with sumptuous Thai and Chinese antiques. Service is definitely a bit ropey for the price range. Also has pool, decent library (free internet) and restaurant.

$$$$ Tamarind Village, 50/1 Rachadamnern Rd, T053-418896, www.tamarindvillage.com. In a great location in the heart of the old city, the Tamarind is a slightly worn and overpriced Lanna-style hotel that caters mostly to package tourists. The gardens and pool are quite pretty though the Lanna boutique vibe is a bit hackneyed.

$$$ 3sis, 1 Soi 8, Prapokklao Rd, T053-273243, www.the3sis.com. This airy, Lanna-style guesthouse consists of 2 buildings and is just across from Wat Chedi Luang. Staff speak excellent English, and rooms are large with a/c, en/suite and TV. Also has Wi-Fi.

$$$ De Lanna, 44 Intawarorot Rd, T053-326266, www.delannahotel.com. Slick, modern Lanna-style hotel with large, stylish rooms. Big soft beds, 32" TV, fridge, safe, funky bathrooms, free Wi-Fi and balcony or terrace. Deluxe rooms have a bathtub as well as a shower. Noise tends to drift up from the often lively central courtyard with swimming pool but this isn't a problem at night. Decent breakfast. Recommended.

$$$ Hotel M, 2-6 Rachdamnern Rd, T053-211070, www.hotelmchiangmai.com. Good central position near Tha Phae Gate, but on an intersection, so tends to be very noisy. Large clean rooms, sparsely furnished, some with a/c. The restaurant, Zest, is one of Chiang Mai's most popular.

$$$ Top North, 41 Moon Muang Rd, T053-279623. Modern hotel in a good location, with pool and decent food. Overpriced – you pay for the location.

$$$ White Chalet Bed & Breakfast, 9/1 Arak Rd, T053-326188, www.chiangmai whitechalet.com. As the name suggests, this guesthouse is all in white, from the chairs in the lobby to the covers on the beds. Fresh-looking standard rooms all come with double bed, flat-screen TV, en suite bathroom and a/c. Earplugs are recommended as the busy (night and day) Arak Rd runs straight past it.

$$$-$$ Rachamankha Flora House, 177/1 Rachamankha Rd, T053-277701, www.rachamankhaflorahouse.com. Homely, friendly upmarket guesthouse in great location. Rooms are airy, nicely designed tiled affairs with a/c and en suite. The upper floors have great views. Breakfast optional and free Wi-Fi. Recommended.

$$ De Rachamankha, 82-86 Rachamankha Rd, T053-278881, www.derachamanka.com. Modern boutique-style guesthouse with 25 rooms around a garden courtyard. Rooms are small but have good facilities: flat-screen TV, Wi-Fi, a/c. Good location in the heart of the old city.

$$ Rendezvous Guesthouse, 3/1 Rachdamnern Soi 5, T053-213763. Situated down a quiet *soi*, good rooms with clean bathrooms, hot showers, cable TV; some rooms have a/c and fridge. Attractive atmosphere with relaxing plant-filled lobby, satellite TV, books and comfy chairs, good value. Very popular with travellers so worth booking in advance.

$ CM Blue House, 30/1 Moonmuang Rd, Soi 6, 053-418512, www.cmbluehouse.com. Friendly guesthouse with attractive garden

area in the laid back northeastern corner of the Old City. A nice budget option with good facilities for the price. Recommended.

$ Eagle House No 2, 26 Rachwithi Rd, Soi 2, T053-210620, www.eaglehouse.com. This is run by an Irish woman, her Thai husband and their friendly, efficient staff. Rooms are clean but a little worn, with a/c or fan and some attached bathrooms. Dorms for ฿100. Excellent food (it is possible to take cookery courses here). Also organizes treks. Recommended.

$ Julie's Guesthouse, 7/1 Phra Pokklao Soi 5, T053-274355, www.julieguesthouse.com. Basic fan rooms, some with their own bathroom and hot water. Friendly atmosphere with lots of communal space for chilling out, including a rooftop. Thai and Western food offered and treks organized. Recommended.

$ Western House Hotel, Soi 5 Sri Phum Rd, T053-215961, www.chiangmaiwestern house.com. One of the best budget places in the entire city. Nicely decorated, simple, clean rooms come with a/c, small balcony (the ones at the front overlook a temple), cable TV and free Wi-Fi. A real find. Little English spoken but friendly and competent. You might need to pay when you check in. Recommended.

Between the eastern city wall and Chang Klang Rd

This area of town includes 2 sections of hotels and guesthouses. On Chang Klang Rd and close by are a number of large, upmarket hotels. The area is busy and noisy (although the hotels need not be), with a good range of restaurants. West of here, down the *sois* or lanes between Loi Kroa and Tha Phae roads, are a number of guesthouses and small mid-range hotels. This area, though quiet and peaceful (usually), is still close to many restaurants and the shops and stalls of Chiang Klang Rd.

$$$$ dusitD2, 100 Chang Klang Rd, T053-999999, www.dusit.com/dusit-d2. Owned by the Dusit Thani chain the D2 attempts to create a designer hotel in the heart of Chiang Mai. However, it doesn't quite pull it off. The rooms, while nicely designed, are small and the over-branded orange-everything is off-putting. However, the food is great and the location, right in the heart of the night market, can't be beaten.

$$$$ Le Meridien Chiang Mai, 108 Chang Klan Rd, T053-253666, www.starwood hotels.com. This huge and unmissable tower block just behind the night market holds a decent 5-star hotel. Pleasant rooms and suites come complete with the usual luxuries and a designer feel. Food in restaurants is not bad either.

$$$$ Mo Rooms, 263/1-2 Tapae Rd, T053-280789, www.morooms.com. Central Chiang Mai boutique meets blank canvas. Named after animals from the Chinese Zodiac, each of the 12 unusually shaped rooms has been decorated by a different Thai artist; raw concrete and flashes of northern artistic brio and whimsy abound. Public areas are equally quirky and there's a small pool. Surprisingly quiet, too, given the location. Recommended.

$$$ Centara Duangtawan Hotel, Loi Kroa Rd, T053-905000, www.centaraduangtawan hotel.com. Great location by the night market and nice rooms for the price. Good facilities, including a decent gym and outdoor pool, a restaurant, bar and shopping on the lower floors, and endless dining, shopping and nightlife options just outside.

$$$ Royal Princess, 112 Chang Klang Rd, T053-253900, www.dusit.com. This 200-room hotel makes an effort to be more Thai than Western in image and style. Service is of a high standard and there's a restaurant, small pool and gym. Of the top-range hotels in town, this is recommended, although its central location on the main road means it's quite noisy.

$$ Lai Thai, 111/4-5 Kotchasan Rd, T053-271725, www.laithai.com. A cross between a north Thai house and a Swiss chalet. Spotless rooms, some with a/c, free baby cots. Popular and professional set-up, good facilities, attractive surroundings, tours,

trekking and motorbike rental. Restaurant, good clean pool. Note that the cheaper rooms at the back are noisy, so expect an early wake-up. Nonetheless, recommended.

$$ Tapae Place Hotel, 2 Tha Phae Soi 3, T053-270159, www.tapaeplacehotel.com. Small mid-range hotel, refined and surprisingly stylish for a place in this price category. Good central location next to Wat Bupharam but set off the busy Tha Phae Rd. A/c, restaurant. Room rate includes breakfast.

$ Kiwi Guesthouse, 54/2 Chang Moi Kao Rd, T08-4406 9982 (mob). Small and friendly guesthouse on a quiet soi. Rooms are clean and simple, with a pleasant seating area outside. Excellent value in a good location. Free Wi-Fi and ping pong.

$ Little Home Guesthouse, 1/1 Kotchasan Soi 3, T053-206939, www.littlehomegh.com. Not a little guesthouse at all, but a large place more like a small hotel. Don't be put off; it is peaceful, down a quiet soi within a leafy compound. The fan or a/c rooms are clean and well maintained, and the management has insisted on no TV, videos or music. Professionally run and popular, with cheap package tours available. Recommended.

$ Namkhong Guesthouse, 55 Tha Phae Soi 3, T053-215556. Friendly guesthouse. All 44 rooms are a little small and can be hot, but they are clean with reasonable attached bathrooms. Treks arranged, restaurant attached, well run and popular.

$ Sarah Guest House, 20 Tha Phae Soi 4, T053-208271, www.sarahgh.hypermart.net. This well-established guesthouse in the heart of the guesthouse area is run by an English woman married to a Thai and is popular. 12 basic but clean rooms, with attached bathrooms and shared hot-water showers. Trekking, tour services and cookery courses. Free Wi-Fi. Recommended.

Near the river

This area includes a number of mid- and upper-range hotels on the river that are within easy walking distance of many restaurants and the shops of Chang Klang Rd.

$$$$ The Chedi, 123 Charoen Prathet Rd, T053-253333, www.ghmhotels.com. A stunningly designed property built around the restored 1920s British consulate – itself a historical treat – has been created here by the river. The rooms are minimalist, with huge tubs and plasma screens while the lobby is spacious with relaxed tones. Pool, sundeck and great food complete the picture. Expensive but almost certainly the best hotel in town. Highly recommended.

$$$ Baan Orapin, 150 Charoenrat Rd, T053-243677, www.baanorapin.com. It is easy to see why this is one of the most popular places in Chiang Mai. A run of well-maintained bungalows surround a central teak house, all set in quiet, gated gardens on a road on the east side of the Ping River. The owner speaks great English and is friendly, though can sometimes be hard to find; it's best to email (see website) or call ahead as **Orapin** is often booked solid.

$$$ Empress Chiang Mai, 199/42 Chang Klang Rd, T053-270240, www.empress hotels.com (see map, page 22). Several restaurants, pool and fitness centre. 375 spacious, attractive rooms with silk wall panelling, carved teakwood furniture and decorated with local products.

$$$ River View Lodge, 25 Soi 2 Charoen Prathet Rd, T053-271109, www.riverview lodgch.com (see map, page 22). Tucked away down a narrow *soi*. A/c, small, family-run, riverside hotel with wonderful gardens, a pool and a friendly vibe. Rooms are overpriced, there's a noisy bar just across the river and service can sometimes be snooty.

$$ Galare Guesthouse, 7 Soi 2 Charoen Prathet Rd, T053-818887, www.galare.com. A/c, restaurant, small hotel in leafy compound, lovely position on the river. Rooms are run-down though service is good and the open-air restaurant, overlooking the Ping, serves simple, tasty food.

$ Kim House, 62 Charoen Prathet Rd, www.kimhousethailand.com, T053-282441. Small hotel in a leafy compound down a secluded soi, with clean rooms (some a/c) and hot showers. Friendly, welcoming atmosphere, and free Wi-Fi. Breakfast included. Recommended.

Nimmanhaemin and Huay Kaew Rd (west of city)

With Nimmanhaemin now firmly established as Chiang Mai's artist quarter a few excellent guesthouses have sprung up. There are also a number of large hotels on Huay Kaew Rd.

$$$$-$$$ Kantary Hills, 44 Nimmanhaemin Rd, Soi 12, T053 222111, www.kantarygroup. com/kantaryhills-chiangmai. This recent stylish addition to Nimman is a nicely crafted hotel-cum-apartment complex with all the mod-cons – roof-top pool, steakhouse restaurant, views of gorgeous Doi Suthep mountain – that any urban hipster has come to expect. There are sleek modernist 1-bedroom apartments and studios, within which you'll find giant flat-screen TVs, Wi-Fi, stereos and even a washing machine. Recommended.

$$$ Casa 2511, 31 Nimmanhaemin Rd, Soi 1, T053-214091, www.casa2511.com. 8 attractive rooms in an old wooden house at the end of one of Nimmenhaemin's trendiest shopping lanes. Friendly staff, a leafy seating area and an excellent café and bakery attached make this a desirable, if a little pricey, place to stay. Free Wi-Fi and breakfast included.

$$$ Chiang Mai Orchid, 23 Huay Kaew Rd, T053-222099, www.chiangmaiorchid.com. Situated right next to the large Kad Suan Kaew shopping complex. Relatively peaceful and attractive hotel, with a/c, pool, health club, efficient service, very good Chinese restaurant. Low-season discounts of up to 50%.

$$$ Yesterday, 24 Nimmanhaemin Rd, T053-213809, www.yesterday.co.th. Opened by the friendly owners of **Baan Say-La**, this beautiful teak house boasts 28 individually designed rooms complete with a/c, en suite and TV, and 2 small houses, as well as free Wi-Fi, breakfast, airport transfer and a garden. Recommended.

$$ Baan Say-La, 4-4/1 Nimmanhaemin Rd, Soi 5, T053-894229, www.baansaylaguest house.com. This cute guesthouse in an old colonial-style building is one of Chiang Mai's best bargains. The tasteful rooms are well designed – some have balconies while everyone has access to the cool air on the roof terrace.

$$ Lotus Hotel Pang Suan Kaew, 21 Huay Kaew Rd, T053-224333, www.lotuspsk hotel.com. This massive hotel is ugly from the outside but makes up for it with competitive rates and large, luxurious rooms. A/c, restaurants, pool and gym.

$ Spicythai Backpackers, 4/80 Nanthawan Village, Nimmanhaemin Rd, T053-400444, www.spicyhostels.com. Set in a small, very quiet compound of houses, **Spicythai** offers a well-managed hostel with dorm rooms. The owner also supplies a range of trips and activities as well as free coffee, tea and internet. You need to be prepared for communal living if you want to stay here – it is slightly reminiscent of the Big Brother house.

Bor Sang and San Kamphaeng circuit
p31

$$ Roong Arun Hot Springs Spa Resort, T053-939128, www.chiangmaihotspring. com. A/c bungalows with pleasant sitting rooms with open fires for the cool season. Access to the resort's swimming pool, jacuzzi, sauna, etc.

Mae Sa Valley–Samoeng circuit *p32*
A number of resorts (**$$$-$$**) have been established along the road around the Doi Suthep-Pui National Park. Most cater for Thais. The largest and most luxurious are **Suan Bua**, in the village of Ban Don, 22 km from Samoeng, T053-365 2709, www.suanbua.com, set in attractively landscaped gardens, and **Belle Villa**, 19 km from Samoeng, T053-365318, www.bellevillaresort.com, where there are cottages for longer-term rental as well as some hotel accommodation.

$$$-$$ Mae Sa Craft Village, T053-290052. A choice of fan and a/c rooms. There's an average restaurant (avoid non-Thai food) and a smallish swimming pool. There are dozens of great activities to get involved in, from ceramic painting to batik dyeing and *sa* paper-making (made from mulberry). There is also a working farm where visitors can help with the rice cultivation, a Thai cookery school and, for people who find all this activity just too exhausting, there's a health centre for massage and relaxation.

Chiang Dao Caves *p34*
$$ Chiang Dao Nest, 144/4 Moo 5 Chiang Dao, T053-456242. www.nest.chiang dao.com. 20 clean and comfortable fan bungalows in a beautiful setting about 2 km from the Chiang Dao caves. Beautiful chill-out gardens, swimming pool, excellent service and free Wi-Fi. The trip from Chiang Mai is worth it for the restaurant alone (see Restaurants, below). Highly recommended.

Lamphun *p34*
$$-$ Phaya Inn, Bann Changkong 35/1, Chitwongpanrangsan Rd, T053-511777, www.phayainn.com. One of the best of the limited options in Lamphun. Clean and modern rooms and attractive gardens. Good location near the Old City and free Wi-Fi.

Lampang *p34*
Because Lampang is only 2 hrs from Chiang Mai, few tourists stay here.
$$$ Lampang River Lodge, 330 Moo 11 Tambon Chompoo, 6 km south of Lampang on the banks of the Wang River, T054-336640, www.lampangriverlodge.com. 60 Thai-style bungalows on stilts in an attractive position, with a/c and restaurant.
$$$ Lampang Wiengthong Hotel, 138/109 Phahonyothin Rd, T054-225801, www.lampangwiengthong.co.th. This is one of the smartest and largest of Lampang's hotels, with 250 a/c rooms, pool, restaurant and free Wi-Fi.

$$ Auangkham Resort, 49-51 Wangnua Rd, T054-221305, www.auangkham lampang.com. This attractive resort on a large garden complex offers a peaceful alternative on the north side of the river. Clean a/c rooms, good facilities, free Wi-Fi and fresh coffee. Good value.

$$ Pin, 8 Suan Dok Rd, T054-221509. A/c, fridge, satellite TV, free Wi-Fi; some rooms have attached bathrooms. Squeaky clean and quiet.

$ Riverside Guesthouse, 286 Talad Kao Rd, T054-227005, www.theriverside-lampang. com. Simple fan or a/c rooms are housed in an old teak complex on the river and individually decorated by the very helpful Italian owner. Family-sized room and suites are also available; most are en suite. The restaurant and terraced communal garden overlooking the Wang River is a lovely chill-out spot. Highly recommended. Free Wi-Fi.

Jai Sorn (Chae Sorn) National Park *p37*

$$ Bungalows are available at the park. Contact the Chae Son National Park, T054-229000, www.dnp.go.th.

Doi Inthanon National Park *p37*
There is a camping ground at the Km 31 mark (₿40 per person). Small tents are available for hire with sleeping bag (₿250 per night).

$$$ Bungalows, Km 31, out-station on the route up the mountain. To book, T02-579 0529 or www.dnp.go.th. Advance reservation recommended as this is a very popular park. A relatively new Karen eco-resort has been set up by 4 villages with support from the National Parks Authorities. The bungalows, sleeping 4-30 people, have been built in the traditional style and the location is fantastic. The resort organizes treks, teaches about medicinal plants, introduces visitors to Karen dance, etc. The resort is on the road to the summit, before the 2nd checkpoint.

Restaurants

For listings of where to go for a northern Khantoke meal plus cultural show, see Entertainment, page 48. Some of the best Thai food, particularly seafood, is served from numerous restaurants, large and small, and countless stalls, in the **Anusarn market** area (see map, page 26). This is the best place to see what is on offer in a small area; food is available all day, but best at night when there is a cacophony of talking, frying and chopping. For food delivery anywhere in and around Chiang Mai from a range of restaurants, check out www.mealsonwheels 4u.com. Note that some bars also serve food; they are listed under Bars and clubs, page 47.

Chiang Mai *p20, maps p22 and p26*
Old City
$$$ Rachamankha, 9 Phra Singh Rd, T053-904114, www.rachamankha.com. (see Where to stay) The restaurant at this stunning hotel serves a tasty menu of Thai and Asian fusion dishes. It is expensive but is a great choice for a romantic splurge.

$$ Brix, Hotel M, Tha Phae Gate, www. hotelmchiangmai.com. Good breakfasts and sandwiches. Nice spot to hang out. Live music in the evenings.

$$ The House, 199 Moon Muang Rd, T053-419011, www.thehousethailand.com. Open 1200-2400. Set in a funky 1930s colonial house, this is an attempt to serve upmarket international and Thai cuisine. It largely succeeds though it is a bit hit and miss. Also includes a cute Moroccan-themed tapas bar.

$$ Jerusalem Falafel, 35/3 Moon Muang Rd, T053-270208. Sat-Thu 0900-2200. Operated by a Thai-Israeli couple, this place doesn't look much from the outside, but don't be put off – it's a cracking little eatery, and the only one of its kind serving a wide variety of very freshly prepared Middle Eastern food. Recommended.

\$\$ Queen Victoria, top of Phra Pokklao Rd, near northern gate, T053-418266. Best British-style home cooking in town. The full cooked breakfast is the best in the north, while the roasts, crumbles and pies should satisfy any homesick Brits. Recommended.

\$\$ UN Irish Pub, 24/1 Rachwithi Rd. Lamb chops, Irish stew, steaks, pasta, lasagne, etc. Pretty good fare in a pub atmosphere. See Bars and clubs, page 47.

\$ The Corner, Rachmanka/Moon Muang Rd. Range of classics and some vegetarian dishes. Also a popular place for breakfast. *Sa* paper products are sold here.

\$ Genchai, 54/1 Sing Ha Rat Rd. Excellent and very popular Isaan and Thai restaurant mostly frequented by locals. Good for sticky rice, grilled catfish and chicken. English menu. Recommended.

\$ SP Chicken, Sri Phum Rd, Open 1500-2200. This local and expat favourite does a roaring trade and that's no surprise. Delicious BBQ meats, spicy salads and surprisingly good thum yam goong (spicy-sour prawn soup). Can be a little hard to spot, look out for the chickens barbecuing outside. Highly recommended.

Between the eastern city wall and Chang Klang Rd

\$\$\$ Moxie, dusitD2 Hotel, 100 Chang Klang Rd, T053-999999, www.dusit.com/dusit-d2. Great breakfasts, lunches and dinners in this designer restaurant. An oasis of calm in the scrum of the night market, this makes a good pit stop. The international and Thai menus are both extensive.

\$\$ Antique House 1, 71 Charoen Prathet Rd (next to the Diamond Riverside Hotel). Open 1100-2400. Well-prepared Thai and Chinese food in a wonderful garden with antiques and an old teak house, built in 1870s (and listed as a National Heritage Site), very nice candlelit ambience, tasty but small servings and rather slow service, live music. Busy road can be intrusive.

\$\$ Art Café, 291 Tha Phae Rd (on the corner facing Tha Phae Gate) T053-206365.

Open 0700-2300. In a great position for trade, this place serves Italian specialities including pizzas and pasta, as well as Thai and Mexican favourites. Fairly expensive.

\$\$ Chez Marco, 15/7 Loi Kroh Rd, T053-207032. Daily 1200-2300. Popular eatery serving up French and European fare. Efficient service and excellent steaks.

\$\$ The Dukes, 49/4-5 Chiang Mai-Lamphun Rd. Daily 1000-2200. Delicious burgers, steaks, pizzas and salads. One of the best places in Chiang Mai for a Western food fix. The pastrami ruben sandwich is a must-try. Also has a restaurant at the night bazaar. Highly recommended.

\$\$ The Gallery, 25-29 Charoenrat Rd, T053-248601, www.thegallery-restaurant.com. Quiet and refined Thai restaurant on the River Ping, in a century-old traditional Thai house with art and crafts gallery attached. Superb food, highly recommended for a special night out. Sit either on a leafy veranda (under an ancient makiang tree) overlooking the river, or inside. Particularly recommended are the fish dishes, including steamed sea bass with lime and deep-fried *plaa chon*.

\$\$ The Good View Bar and Restaurant, 13 Charoenrat Rd, T053-249029. Not open for lunch. Situated on the Ping River, outdoor or a/c dining available. Good live music and bar and very reasonably priced. The atmosphere is more modern than its long-established neighbour, the Riverside Restaurant, and it is frequented by Chiang Mai's yuppies.

\$\$ Miguels, 106/1 Chaiyaphum Rd, T053-874148, www.miguels-cafe.com. Daily 1000-2300. Good, lively atmosphere in this friendly and well-run Mexican diner. Huge choice of enchiladas and burritos and massive side orders. Popular with expat community.

\$\$ Pulcinella da Stefano, 2/1-2 Chiang Mai Kao Rd, T053-874189. Daily 1100-2300. Good Italian-owned restaurant just a stone's throw from Tha Phae Gate. Extensive selection of pizzas, pastas and salads in a relaxed atmosphere. Recommended.

$$ The Riverside, 9-11 Charoenrat Rd, T053-243239, www.theriversidechiang mai.com. A staircase at the back of this rambling teak house leads down to one of the city's favourite riverside terraces. The Thai, northern Thai and European food hits the spot, especially among tourists, but locals also know it as one of Chiang Mai's best live music venues, with acoustic duos and bands from 1900 each night. Very busy at weekends. Prompt waiters read back your orders to avoid those all-to-common misunderstandings.

$$ Spicy Bollywood, Chiayaphum Rd, opposite Somphet Market. Daily 1200-2200. Tucked a little bit back from the road, this is one of the better Indian restaurants in town and not too expensive. Good curries, fresh naans and friendly service. All-you-can-eat buffet every Fri night.

$ Aroon Rai, 43-45 Kotchasan Rd. Open 0900-2200. Very big restaurant, good-value Thai food, north Thai specialities, very popular. Tables on the open-air upper floor are quieter.

$ Mike's, corner of Chang Moi and Chaiyaphum Rd. Daily 1200-0200. Created by an American expat, **Mike's** serves up burgers, fries and shakes. You can sit at the retro road-side bar or take away.

$ Tea House Siam Celadon, 158 Tapae Rd, T053-242 292. The front of this old colonial-style white house, with its gently rotating ceiling fans and ornate wood fretwork, flogs ceramics, while the tea shop occupies the conservatory and leafy garden out back. Service can be shambling but it's a soothing spot for snacks and a good cuppa.

West bank of the river off Charoen Prathet Rd

$$$ The Restaurant, The Chedi, 123 Charoen Prathet Rd, T053-253333, www.ghm hotels.com. You'll find great traditional northern Thai specialities and innovative Pacific Rim cuisine complemented by an extensive wine list served in what was once the British consulate – it also serves afternoon tea. Expensive but recommended.

$ Sophia, Charoen Prathet Soi 1 (down a narrow *soi* between the night market and the river road). Cheap and very popular Muslim restaurant, this *soi* also usually supports a number of stalls, serving Malay/ Muslim dishes from roti to mutton curry.

Nimmanhaemin Rd and Huay Kaew Rd (west of city)

$$$ La Casa, Chonlapratan Rd T053-215802, just north of Huay Kaew Rd. Set in an attractive wooden house, good range of authentic Italian cuisine (heavy on the garlic), apparently a popular restaurant with the Queen of Thailand. Fairly pricey.

$$$ Mi Casa, 28 Nimmanhaemin Soi 11, T08-0033 2825, www.micasachiangmai. com. Mediterranean food served in a beautiful homely setting. A good selection of tapas, wine and vegetarian dishes makes this restaurant a favourite with the hip Thai crowd.

$$ Amazing Sandwich, 202 Huey Kaew Rd. Mon-Sat 0900-1800, Sun 0900-1600. Probably the best sandwiches in Chiang Mai. Great range of breads, rolls and fillings, so you can create your own masterpiece. Good breakfast, lunch and pizza menu as well. Recommended.

$$ Hong Tauw Inn, 95/16-17 Nimmanhaemin Rd, T053-400039. Elegant restaurant with an antique clock collection, relaxed, friendly service, northern Thai specialities from regional sausage to crispy catfish, plus ice-cold beer. Slightly more expensive than the average Thai restaurant. Recommended.

$$ Khun Churn, 136/28 Nimmanhaemin Rd. Soi 17, T053-224124. Seriously tasty Thai vegetarian food in a relaxed open-air setting. The daily all-you-can-eat lunch buffet is cheap and has a loyal following. Recommended.

$$ The Salad Concept, 49/9-10 Nimmanhaemin Rd (corner of Soi 13), T053-894455.Open 1100-2200. Cute mustard-green café serving huge build-your-own salads as well as organic juices like the 'Anticancer', a refreshing blend of wheatgrass, guava, apple, celery and ginger. Popular and cheap, with fast service. Recommended.

$ Cat House, Siri Mangkalajarn Lane 3, T086-1968422, www.cathouse-cm.com. A true fusion restaurant. The owner Jackie serves whatever she feels like, from chicken curry with mango chutney sandwiches to exhibitions, yoga and shaking meditation classes.

$ Pun Pun, Wat Suan Dok, Suthep Rd, www.punpunthailand.org. This Thai vegetarian restaurant in the grounds of Wat Suan Dok serves organic food made with ingredients bought from nearby cooperative farms. Beautiful setting, popular with monks and the local expat crowd. Highly recommended.

$ Tsunami Sushi Bar, Huay Kaew Rd, opposite Lanna Condo II. Daily 1730-2330. Quality, affordable Japanese food. Very popular with students, so you may have to wait for a seat. Highly recommended.

Elsewhere in the city

$$$ Le Coq d'Or, 68/1 Koh Klang Rd, www.lecoqdorchiangmai.com, T053-141555. A long-established international restaurant, set in a pleasant house. Over-zealous waiters anticipate your every need. High standard of cuisine (including mouth-watering steaks), choice of wines, not heavily patronized, pricey.

$$ Ruen Come-In, 79/3 Srithon Rd, www.ruencomein.com, T053-212516, Chang Puak, down a *soi* opposite Wat Jet Yod. Set in a traditional teak house and pleasant garden, not easy to locate.

Around Chiang Mai *p29*
Anusarn Market, southeast of night market has foodstalls. These are mostly open at night, but a smaller number are open throughout the day, they're cheap (฿25-30 single-dish meals), lively and fun. Chang Klang Rd has stalls selling delicious

pancakes, ฿15-20; **Somphet Market** (see map, page 26), Moon Muang Rd, is good for takeaway curries, fresh fish, meat and fruit!; and north of **Chang Phuak Gate**, outside the moat, is another congregation of good foodstalls. **Warorot Market**, north of Chang Klang and Tha Phae roads, is a great place for foodstalls at night.

If you need a/c comfort, then there are some excellent food courts in the basement of the **Airport Plaza** and **Pang Suan Kaew** (aka Central), Huay Kaew Rd. The former is quieter and slightly less frenetic than Pang Suan Kaew, which is a bit like eating in a crowd of pedestrians. Buy coupons (any you don't spend can be redeemed) and then browse the stalls: wide range of noodle and rice dishes, drinks, *kanom*, Korean, Japanese and some other Asian cuisines, along with cold drinks including bottled and draft beer.

$$$ Le Crystal, 74/2 Paton Rd, www.le crystalrestaurant.com, T053-872890. A top-class French dining experience on the banks of the Ping River a little out of town. Excellent service and great food. Highly recommended.

$$$ Palaad Tawanron Restaurant, Suthep Rd (near university), T053-217 073, www.palaadtawanron.com. Set on the lower parts of the Doi Suthep mountain near a large waterfall and amid thick forest, this is an award-winning restaurant. Book a terrace table at the back and you'll also secure an awesome view to go with your sundowner. **Palaad** also offers some of the best Thai food in Chiang Mai. Highly recommended.

$$ Galae, 65 Suthep Rd, T053-278655. In the foothills of Doi Suthep on the edge of a reservoir, west of the city, Thai and northern Thai dishes in a beautiful garden setting.

Chiang Dao *p33*
$$$ Chiang Dao Nest, www.nest.chiang dao.com (see Where to stay, above). Daily 1000-2130. Delicious European gourmet food in a wonderful natural setting. From starter to dessert, there is nothing on the menu that disappoints. Good selection of

wines and great service. Excellent value and easily the best restaurant for miles. Highly recommended.

Lamphun *p34*
There are some reasonable foodstalls around Wat Phra That Haripunjaya while on the road running down the south wall of the monastery is **Lamphun Ice**, an a/c place good for ice cream, coffee and a 16-page menu with delicacies such as pig's knuckle and chicken tendon. For Kuaytiaw fans, there is a tremendous **Duck Noodle Soup Shop** on Inthayongyot Rd, just south of Wat Phra That Haripunjaya.

Lampang *p34*
For a cheap meal, try one of the Thai pavement cafés along Ropwiang Rd between the clock tower and the **Lampang Guesthouse**. There are foodsatlls near the railway station and around the market.
$$ Riverside (Baan Rim Nam), 328 Tipchang Rd. Wooden house overlooking the river, attractive ambience, reasonable Thai and international food. Recommended.
$ Oey Thong Café, Tipchang Rd (near the bridge). Good Thai food in cosy surroundings.
$ Aroy One Baht, 297 Tipchang Rd. Top-notch Thai food on 2 levels in an attractive old wooden house. Extremely popular with locals, and quite probably the best *pad phak boong* (fried morning glory) to be found in town.

Doi Inthanon National Park *p37*
A small shop at the Km 31 mark will serve meals. There are no stalls on the summit, although there is a restaurant near the *chedis* close to the summit.

🎵 Bars and clubs

Chiang Mai *p20, maps p22 and p26*
Chiang Mai has a reasonable bar scene but is fairly subdued compared to Bangkok – there is the usual run of go-go bars along **Loi Kroa Rd**. If nothing grabs you from the list

below there is a smattering of usually short-lived hip bohemian hang-outs scattered throughout the Old City particularly along **Rachdamnern** and **Rachwithi** roads. The area around **Tha Phae Gate** also has a high concentration of watering holes. There are quite a few pubs at the western end of **Loi Kroa Rd**. A younger, hipper Thai crowd – and a few *farang* – hang out at various generic nightspots along **Nimmanhaemin Rd**. However, you'll need to search the back sois to find the best places.
FabriQue Club, President Hotel, 226 Wichayanont Rd. A large, loud nightclub, extremely popular with both Westerners and Thais, though 'farang' must pay a ฿300 cover charge.
Lost Hut, 3/1 Moon Muang Soi 1. Canadian and Thai-owned bar at the end of a quiet soi. Good music and a laidback atmosphere make it an ideal spot for a relaxing beer.
Rasta Café, Charoen Prathet Rd. Between the night market and iron bridge, this is the hang-out of choice for the toking traveller set. Expect dub, reggae, roots, recorded and live. More scruffy bars nearby.
Roof Top, Kotchasan Rd, just down from Tha Phae Gate, and accessed through the **Tribal Hemp Connection** shop. A seriously laid-back setting, the roof pulls back to create a breezy atmosphere, where countless mats, cushions and low tables play host to a merry band of travellers. Very popular.
UN Irish Pub, Rachwithi Rd. Open 0900-2400. Good atmosphere and cheap food available (see Restaurants, above). The name speaks for itself – management (which is Australian) help to organize the (small) annual St Patrick's Day parade. Quiz nights, live music and occasionally English Premiership football.
Warm-Up Café, 40 Nimmanhaemin Rd, T053-400-676. Open 1800-0100. Popular club, bar and restaurant attracting a young crowd of trendy Thai students and expats. Live music and DJ.
Zoe in Yellow, Rachwithi Rd. The centre-piece of a cluster of bars within the Old City. A backpacker favourite.

Lampang *p34*

There are a few options along Tipchang Rd, which can get fairly lively at the weekends; some bars offer live music.

Relax, Tipchang Rd (next to **Riverside Restaurant**). Modern-style bar in wooden building overlooking the river. Cold beer and more, open-air veranda.

Riverside (see Restaurants, above). Live music most nights, ranging from rock and roll to romantic Thai ballad groups.

⏺ Entertainment

Chiang Mai *p20, maps p22 and p26*
Cinema
Chiang Mai University Art Center (see page 28), free foreign independent movies on Sat evenings.

Kad Suan Gaew Shopping Mall, Huay Kaew Rd. Top floor, 3 screens, latest blockbusters, changes every Fri. ฿80. Call 'Movieline' for information, T053-262661.

Major Cineplex, 4th floor, Airport Plaza Shopping Mall, Hwy 1141 (on the way to the airport), T053-283939, www.major cineplex.com. Big cinema complex, showing American blockbusters and the latest Thai movies. ฿120.

Cultural centres
Alliance Française, 138 Charoen Prathet Rd, T053-275277. Presents French cultural (and some northern Thai) activities, including screening of French films with English subtitles.

American University Alumni (AUA), 24 Rachdamnern Rd, T053-278407. Library Mon-Fri 1200-1800, Sat 0900-1200. English and Thai classes; films and other shows.

British Council, 198 Bumrungrat Rd, T053-242103, www.britishcouncil.org.

Cultural shows and Khantoke dinners
These traditional northern Thai meals get a lot of coverage. Average food is served at low tables by traditionally dressed women while diners sit on the floor. In addition to the one listed below, **Diamond Riverside Hotel**, Charoen Prathet Rd, and the **Galare Food Centre**, in the night bazaar, Chang Klang Rd, also organize Khantoke dinners.

Old Chiang Mai Cultural Centre, 185/3 Wualai Rd, T053-202993, www.oldchiang mai.com. Admission ฿650 (book in advance), Khantoke dinner, followed by hilltribe show, daily 1900-2130.

Horse racing
Next to the Lanna Public Golf Course, Chotana Rd (4 km north of the city). Races every Sat, 1200-1730.

Muay Thai (Thai boxing)
Kawila Boxing Stadium, near Nawarat Bridge. Fri from 2000. For ฿400 you'll see 10 matches between both foreign and Thai boxers, as well as rowdy locals placing illegal bets (betting is outlawed in Thailand). Tickets can be purchased at the stadium or from travel agents in town.

⏺ Festivals

Chiang Mai *p20, maps p22 and p26*
Jan Chiang Mai Winter Fair, 10-day festival held late Dec/early Jan, based in the Municipal Stadium. Exhibitions, Miss Beauty Contest, musical performances.

Mid-Jan Bor Sang Umbrella Fair (outside Chiang Mai) celebrates traditional skills of umbrella-making, and features contests, exhibitions and stalls selling umbrellas and other handicrafts. Miss Bor Sang, a beauty contest, is also held.

1st weekend in Feb Flower Festival. This is a great festival and is centred on the inner moat road, at the southwest corner of the Old City, where small displays of flowers and plants are arranged by schools, colleges and professional gardeners and garden shops from across the north. There are also, as you would expect in Thailand, lots of foodstalls as well as handicrafts. If you have ever felt the urge to grow a papaya tree, then this is the place to get your seeds. The highlight is a parade of floral floats along with the requisite beauty contest. If you want to avoid the crowds, come on the Fri evening.

13-16 Apr Songkran, traditional Thai New Year (public holiday) celebrated with more gusto in Chiang Mai than elsewhere. Boisterous water-throwing, particularly directed at *farangs*; expect to be soaked to the skin for the entire 4 days.

Mid-Nov Yi Peng Loi Krathong, a popular Buddhist holiday when *krathong* (boats) filled with flowers and lit candles are floated down the river. Fireworks at night, and small hot-air balloons are launched into the sky.

1st week Dec Nimmanhaemin Arts Festival. Pleasant Soi 1 is closed to traffic and given over to the best of Chiang Mai's designers in what is rapidly becoming on northern Thailand's premium arts festivals.

Lampang *p34*
Feb (movable) Luang Wiang Lakon, 5 important Buddha images are carried through the streets in procession. Theremis traditional dancing and a light show at Wat Lampang Luang.

◎ Shopping

Chiang Mai *p20, maps p22 and p26*
Chiang Mai is a shoppers' paradise. It provides many of the treasures of Bangkok, in a compact area. The craft 'villages' on the San Kamphaeng and Hang Dong (Ban Tawai) roads are a popular jaunt of the coach tour, whilst the night market, with its array of handicrafts, antique shops and fake designer shirts, continues to pack the tourists in night after night. A quieter, less frequented spot, is the group of sophisticated shops, cafés and bars, that have opened up in the lanes off Nimmanhaemin Rd, mostly patronized by trendy Thai students and the expat crowd. Soi 1 and Soi 4 in particular (where Nimman Promenade is located) are both great little alleys featuring small design boutiques, galleries and coffee shops. Tha Phae Rd is an old favourite and is smartening up its act,

with the likes of **Senses** and **Contemporary Jewellery** opening up. Two department stores at Kad Suan Kaew on Huay Kaew Rd and the Airport Plaza, south of town near the airport, provide focal points for a vast array of shops, including plenty of cheap clothes outlets. The area around Tha Phae Gate becomes pedestrianized on a Sun afternoon and evening to make way for hundreds of food and souvenir stalls and buskers.

If you want to ship your goodies back home, **DHL** has an office in the Old City right next to Tha Phae Gate; **UPS** has a walk-in office at 77 Sri Phum Rd, inside the moat near Changpuak Gate, T053-416351, Mon-Sat 0830-1730.

Antiques and lacquerware
There are a number of shops on **Tha Phae Rd**. Another good road to wander along is Loi Kroa, which supports a many antique and hilltribe handicraft shops. **Hang Dong Rd** has several places worth a browse, as does the **San Kamphaeng Rd**, towards Bor Sang (to get there, take a tuk-tuk or a bus from the north side of Charoen Mang Rd). Beware of fakes. Cheaper lacquerware is available from the night bazaar.

La Luna, set on the eastern side of the Ping River at 190 Charoenrat Rd, www.laluna gallery.com. One of a growing number of contemporary art galleries opening up in Chiang Mai. This airy, open-plan space, houses abstract works and photography from throughout Southeast Asia. They also sell a range of high-quality gifts and prints.

Sanpranon Antiques, west side of Hang Dong Rd, about 4 km from Airport Plaza. Set off the road in a traditional Thai house, it's a huge place well worth a visit just to rummage about. There's an overwhelming amount of stock (from lacquerware to ceramics to woodcarvings), much of which is clearly not antique, but it's fun to nose.

Art galleries
Chiang Mai is generously sprinkled with some of the best modern art being made

in Southeast Asia today. Read the local papers, such as *Chiang Mai City Life* (www.chiangmainews.com) and check out the sois around Nimmanheimin and Charoenrat roads for news about exhibitions. Small new galleries seemingly open and close at a whim.
La Luna, 190 Charoenrat Rd, eastern side of the Ping River, T053-306678, www.laluna gallery.com. One of a growing number of contemporary art galleries in Chiang Mai. This airy, open-plan space houses abstract works and photography from throughout Southeast Asia. They also sell a range of high-quality gifts, sculptures and prints.
Suvannabhumi Art Gallery,
116 Chareonrat Rd, T081-031 5309 (mob), www.suvannabhumiartgallery.com. A high-calibre modern art gallery featuring the work of prominent artists from Burma exclusively. Visiting this transplanted gallery space, you benefit from not only the owner's excellent taste, but also her deep connections with the Burmese arts scene. Not to be missed.

Bookshops

Backstreet Books, 2/8 Chiang Moi Kao Rd, www.backstreetbooks.com. Right next door to Gecko near Tha Phae Gate, this Irish-owned bookshop offers an extensive selection across many languages. Friendly and helpful owner.
Book Zone, 318 Tha Phae Rd, part of **Asia Books**. Open 0900-2130. This small store sells Thai coffee-table books, a good range of guidebooks, some English-language novels, children's books, magazines and maps. The main branch of **Gecko Books**, www.geckobooks.net, is near Thae Pae Gate at 2/6 Chang Moi Kao Rd. The other 3 branches are at 2 Rachamanka Rd, 2 Chaiyaphum Rd and 80 Loi Kroa Rd. Big selection of new and used books in English, Dutch, German, French, Swedish, Danish and Norwegian.

Ceramics and terracotta

Beautiful celadon-glazed ceramics can be found in proliferation in Chiang Mai. **San Kamphaeng Rd** is as good a place as any to see a number of set-ups. Several of the establishments on this road are selling outlets for small factories on the same site, which are open to visitors. One such place is:
Baan Celadon, 7 Moo 3, Chiangmai-Sankamphaeng Rd, T053-338288. A good range of ceramics for sale from simple everyday bowls to elaborate vases.
Mengrai Kilns, 79/2 Arak Rd, T053-272063. A showroom only, with a good range of celadon-ware. Seconds at reasonable prices.
Siam Celadon, 38 Moo 10, Sankampaeng Rd, T053-331526. Award-winning designs though it is a little far from town.

Clothes

A huge assortment of T-shirts, cotton clothing and tribal clothing can be found in the 3 night markets on **Chang Klang Rd**. Other shops along **Tha Phae Rd** or for more contemporary styles, the 2 shopping centres (**Kad Suan Kaew** on Huay Kaew Rd and **Airport Plaza**) have a good range. The former has some bargains on both the top and basement floors. If you want to have clothes made to measure, see Tailors, below. See also Silk, lace and textiles, below.
Ginger Shop, 199 Moon Muang, T053-419 011. Sells a wide range of clothes and accessories for both men and women. Chic and beautiful, but expensive and somewhat exclusive.
Kad Suan Kaew, Huay Kaew Rd. This is the place to come for cheap clothes. Lots of small shops and stalls mostly concentrated on the top floor, with a few more in the basement and scattered through the complex.

Computers and software

Panthip Plaza, 152/1 Changklan Rd, is the Chiang Mai version of the Bangkok classic. Everything any computer could ever want – mounds of hardware and mountains of software. Pick up the latest PC and Mac programme copies at a fraction of the published cost.

Furniture and rattanware

If you are prepared to ship furniture home, Chiang Mai is an excellent place to rummage around for it. For locally made products, Hang Dong Rd is your best bet, with plenty of choice (and they can make furniture to order too). The best area to look is immediately to the east of Hang Dong – turn left at the junction. There is a strip of shops along here selling an excellent range of furniture, both old and new. The road to Bor Sang (the San Kamphaeng Rd, to the northeast of town) is also worth a visit. There are also quite a few shops selling furniture imported from the region. For rattanware there is a good range of cheaper stalls strung out along Route 108 towards Hang Dong, about 10 km south of town. Some of the best rattan shops in the inner city are located on Chiang Moi Rd, just east of the Old City. See also Interior design, below.

Hang Dong Rattan, Loi Kroa Rd (near intersection with Kamphaeng Din Rd). High-quality rattan products.

Under the Bo, 22-23 Night Bazaar, also has a shop on the west side of Hang Dong Rd, about 4 km south of the Airport Plaza. Fascinating mixture of Indonesian, Bhutanese, Afghan and Pakistani pieces. Worth a visit.

Hilltribe textiles and handicrafts

Chiang Mai is the centre for hilltribe items. There is a bewildering array of goods, much of which is of poor quality (Tha Phae Rd seems to specialize in a poorer range of products). Bargain for everything. The night market on Chang Klang Rd has a lot on offer but better pieces can be found at the more exclusive shops on Loi Kroa Rd.

Kesorn Arts, 154-156 Tha Phae Rd, T053-874325. One of the biggest stashes of old hilltribe fabrics in town, some of them dating back to the early 19th century. Recommended.

Thai Tribal Crafts, 208 Bumrungrat Rd, near McCormick Hospital, T053-241043, www.ttcrafts.co.th. Run by Karen and Lahu church organizations on a non-profit basis. Good selection, quality and prices.

Homewares

Chakhriya, 14/7 Nimman Promenade, Nimmanhaemin Rd, T08-1952 5773 (mob). Cosy boutique selling everything for the home.

Gong Dee, 30 Nimmaneheimen Soi 1, T053-225032, www.gongdeegallery.com. Famous for the gold leaf decorating most products, this repository of beautiful paintings, carvings and homewares was here long before Nimmaneheimen became hip. Occasionally hosts exhibitions by local artists. Recommended.

Interior design

Chiang Mai is undoubtedly the best place outside Bangkok to find good-quality 'decorative items' and contemporary furniture for your home. Probably the best concentration of shops of this kind is on Nimmanhaemin Rd, but Charoenrat Rd is also well worth a visit.

Aesthetic Accessories, 50-60 Rachmanka Rd, opposite Anodard Hotel, T053-278659. This is a great little place selling beautiful small-scale 'accessories'. Quite pricey by Thai standards.

Nara, 14/30 Nimman Promenade, Nimmanhaemin Rd. Chic decor shop, specializing in lamps in unique and modern designs. Quite pricey for Thai standards.

Villa Cini, 30, 32 and 34 Charoenrat Rd, T053-244025. Beautiful range of textiles and antiques, high-quality products displayed in sophisticated surroundings makes for inflated prices, but it's fun to browse here. Also has a small restaurant in the courtyard.

Jewellery and silverwork

Chiang Mai now offers not only a proliferation of hilltribe jewellery, but also some better quality, contemporary designed jewellery. A good starting point is Tha Phae Rd.

For more traditional, Thai-style silverwork, make your way to Wualai Rd which runs off the southern moat road. There are quite a number of shops and workshops down here on both sides of the road.

Contemporary Jewellery, 201 Tha Pha Rd, T053-273058. Contemporary custom-made gold and silver jewellery by Thai and Western designers.

Old Silver, 59/3 Loi Kroa Rd, and **Sipsong Panna Silver**, 95/19 Nimmanhaemin Rd. Both sell traditional and modern silver jewellery.

Senses, 276/278 Tha Phae Rd, T053-874299. A good range of modern silver jewellery in an old Thai wooden house. There's no sign on this shop, but it's directly opposite the K-Bank.

Night markets

Situated on the west and east sides of Chang Klang Rd, Chiang Mai's multiple night markets are now a major tourist attraction and consist of 2- or 3-storey purpose-built structures containing countless stalls. It is an excellent place to browse and, along with a wide range of tribal handicrafts, it is possible to buy T-shirts, watches, cheap CDs, leather goods, children's clothes and Burmese 'antiques'. In addition, there are some better-quality shops selling jewellery, antiques and silks (both ready-made and lengths) on the 1st floor of the Viang Ping Building. Most stalls and shops open at about 1800 and close around 2300.

Huay Kaew Rd night market, north of Nimmanhaemin Rd. Daily 1800-2300. Caters mainly to students and offers cheap clothes, shoes, accessories, and food.

Mae Jo, 287 Chiang Mai-Mae Jo Rd. Sells fresh food, plants and household items.

Warorot Market, north of Tha Phae Rd. Open 0700-1600. Clothing, fabric, sportswear, hilltribe handicrafts.

Wualai Rd, south of the moat, turns into a walking street on Sat 1700-2300. Here you can find everything from cheap clothing and home-made jewellery to art, make-up and kitchenware. Popular with locals.

Paper products

There is now a proliferation of shops selling handmade paper products. The best place to find paper is along San Kamphaeng Rd, where there are many small-scale operations making paper. Take the lane to the west just before Chiang Mai Sudaluck, and before the Bor Sang junction.

Silk, lace and textiles

For a good range of textiles, it is worth walking down Loi Kroa Rd, east of the city wall.

Classic Lanna Thai, night bazaar, upper floor, far right-hand corner. Fabulous range of well-designed jackets, dresses and blouses. Also sells antique silk. Will make to measure.

Nandakwang, 6/1-3 Nimmanhaemin Rd, T053-222261, also 3rd floor, **Chiang Inn Plaza**, Chiang Klan Rd, T053-281356. Loose-weave cotton 'homespun creations', ranging from napkins to cushion covers to bedspreads to made-up clothing. Attractive range of colours. Also some ceramics (brightly coloured coffee cups).

Shinawatra Silk, Huay Kaew Rd (opposite **Chiang Mai Orchid Hotel**). For the usual array of silk products: specs cases, silk frames, ties, scarves, and endless bolts of fabric. Hardly funky, but a good stop for stocking fillers for the grandparents/parents.

Supermarkets and department stores

Central Department Store, in the Kad Suan Kaew shopping complex on Huay Kaew Rd and the **Airport Plaza** shopping complex southwest of the Old City. Both also have **Tops** supermarkets in their basements, which are good for Western food.

Lotus/Tesco, Hang Dong Rd, about 3 km south of **Airport Plaza**. Enormous place selling household goods, clothing, electrical goods and a big supermarket, with a good range of fresh fruit and vegetables and some Western foods. There is also a large **Tesco Lotus** on the Superhighway.

Rimping Supermarket. This fastgrowing Chiang Mai chain of small supermarkets is the best for Western foods (including good cheeses, salads, cold meats and pâtés). More accessible branches to be found off Chotana Rd and Charoenrat Rd (near the Iron Bridge).

Tailors

Many of the stalls in and around Warorot Market will make up clothes. Walk north along Vichayanon Rd from Tha Phae Rd. **Big Boss**, 99/8 Loi Kroh Rd, T053-818953. Friendly staff and a fantastic range of silks.

Woodcarving

Western tastes are accommodated for along Tha Phae Rd, with many outlets selling carved wooden trinkets.

Ban Tawai is a woodcarving centre about 3 km east of Hang Dong (itself 15 km south of town). This place began life as a woodcarving village, and has been colonized and now has shops and stalls selling everything from cheap and cheerful frogs to grandiose sculptures. Packing services available.

Ratana House, 284 Chiang Mai-Hang Dong Rd, east side, T053-271734. Huge range of goods from Burmese lacquerware to wood products of all descriptions – both large (chests and cupboards) and small (candlesticks and wooden frogs).

Lampang *p34*
Ceramics

Lampang is famous for its ceramics. There are more than 50 factories in and around the town; a number are to be found to the west along Phahonyothin Rd and Rte 1 towards Ko Kha (eg, **Art Lampang**).

Handicrafts

Lampang Plaza, on Ropwiang Rd near the clock tower, sells an assortment of knick-knacks like wind chimes, shells and ceramics from a series of stalls.

Northern Handicraft Hilltribe Shopping Centre, a small teak house and, unfortunately, not as grand as it sounds.

Chiang Mai *p20, maps p22 and p26*
Latest information on sports is listed in most free newspapers and newsletters, available from many shops, hotels and guesthouses. Any tour operator will offer a range of activities and tours to choose from. Here are a few of the highlights.

Boat trips

Evening departures from the **Riverside Restaurant** on Charoenrat Rd for trips on the Ping River. ฿110 a head.

Bungee jumping

Jungle Bungy Jump, T053-297700, www.junglebungy.com.

Cookery courses

Baan Thai, 11 Rachdamnern Rd, Soi 5, T053-357 339, www.cookinthai.com. All day hands-on lesson for ฿900. Provides free transportation to and from your guesthouse.

Chiang Mai Thai Cookery School, book through 47/2 Moon Muang Rd (opposite Tha Phae Gate). T053-206388, www.thai cookeryschool.com. One of the best. Runs a variety of courses from ฿1450 for 1 day.

Eagle II Guesthouse, 26 Rachwithi Rd, Soi 2 (see Where to stay, above). Also runs recommended cookery courses.

Siam Rice Thai Cookery School, 211 Moo 13 Soi 5 Canal Rd, T053-329091, www.siam ricethaicookery.com. Half-day, full-day and evening classes featuring English speaking instructors and a visit to the local market.

You Sabai Home, Baan Thai Project, Mae Teang, T085-7206201, www.yousabai.com. Lovely Yao and her husband, both fluent English-speakers, offer 4-day organic vegetarian cooking courses, run from their farm in You Sabai. Stay in simple earthen huts, participate in yoga or just enjoy the stunning scenery around their farm. Recommended. Costs ฿3200.

Cycling

Website www.chiangmaicycling.org covers Chiang Mai's cycling routes, bicycle hardware/rental shops and tour operators. Several shops near Tha Phae Gate and along Loi Kroa Rd rent out bikes, as do some guesthouses. A deposit or a copy of your passport will probably be required.

Fitness and sports centres

700 Year Stadium, Canal Rd, 0900-2000, ฿30-90. There is a good gym and weights area in the swimming pool section of this huge sports complex, built to accommodate the 1997 ASEAN games. 6 km out of town, so not practical unless you have your own transport.

Centara Duangtawan Hotel, Loi Kroa Rd (see Where to stay), T053-905000. Modern gym and outdoor swimming pool. Excellent monthly rates.

Hash House Harriers, Hash Pub, 129 Kampangdin Rd, opposite the Mae Ping Hotel. T053-449695, www.hashpub.com. Hashes every week.

Hillside Fitness Centre, 4th floor, Hillside Plaza 4, Huay Kaew Rd, T053-225984. Fitness centre, sauna and herbal steam rooms, beauty treatment.

Golf

Golf has seen something of a renaissance in recent years with an excellent choice of courses to suit all budgets. Information on golf courses in and around Chiang Mai can be found at www.chiangmaigolf.com.

Gassan Lake City, Lamphun. A challenging course in a beautiful setting south of Chiang Mai. Green fee ฿2600, ฿2900 at weekends. Club hire from ฿600.

Lanna Public Golf Course, Chotana Rd (at Nong Bua, 4 km north of the city). Open 0600-1930. A woodland course. Green fee ฿800, ฿1000 at weekends, club hire ฿500. There is also a driving range here.

Horse riding

Chiang Mai Horse Riding, T053-874091, www.horseriding.chiangmaiinfo.com. Offers a range of trips for beginners and experienced riders near scenic Huay Tung Tao lake.

Lanna Sports Centre, Chotana Rd (north of town), ฿250 per hr, call Janet, T053-217956.

Meditation, t'ai chi and yoga

Namo Chiang Mai, 109/1 Moon Muang Soi 4, T053-326648, www.namochiang mai.com. A choice of daily yoga classes in a convenient location in the Old City. Massage and massage courses also available. Recommended.

T'ai Chi Chuan, 3/7 Rattana Kosin Rd, Soi 1, T085-7145537 (mob), www.taichi thailand.com. 40-hr introductory courses start on the 1st and 16th day of each month. Advanced classes available by appointment. Accommodation available.

Mountain biking

Click and Travel Ltd, T053-281553, www.clickandtravelonline.com. Soft adventure company specializing in bicycle tours. As well as guided tours, they also offer a self-guided option that allows you to go it alone (with back-up if necessary).

Mountain Biking Chiang Mai, 1 Samlan Rd, T081-024 7046 (mob), www.mountain bikingchiangmai.com. Well-organized outfit offering an extensive range of bike trips, ranging from easy to intermediate, along roads and dirt tracks around Chiang Mai's Doi Suthep and other lofty peaks in the region. Most outings are 1 day, but some 2-day trips also available. Prices range from about ฿1500 to ฿5000.

Swimming

700 Year Stadium, Canal Rd (see above). There's an Olympic-size pool here for serious swimmers. Open 0900-2000, ฿60.

Lotus-Pang Suan Kaew Hotel, see Where to stay. Has a big rooftop pool, 0900-2100 (฿100).

Tennis

700 Year Stadium, see above. Well maintained courts. Instruction available too.

Therapies and massage

There are umpteen places in town offering massage. They tend to charge around the same amount (฿200 per hr). Note that many masseuses seem to have had rudimentary training and the massage rooms consist of mattresses laid on the floors of upper rooms. The experience may be pleasant enough, but don't expect your sinuses to clear or your lower colon to sort itself out. For a traditional Thai massage, it is best to avoid the places geared to tourists around Tha Phae Gate.

In an unusual rehabilitation initiative, **Chiang Mai's women's jail**, sited at 100 Ratchawithi Rd in the middle of the old city, has opened a spa (T081-706 1041) staffed entirely by female prisoners. Here, the paying public can get body and foot massages, herbal steam and a variety of beauty treatments. Daily 0800-1630. A foot massage costs ฿150 per hr, a body massage ฿180. Almost all of the money goes directly to the masseuse, helping them to get ready for when they are released.

Fah Lanna, 186/3 Loy Kroh Rd, T082-030 3029 (mob), www.fahlanna.com. Cheap, cosy exotic little spa 5-mins' walk from the night market. Recommended.

Oasis Spa, 102 Sirimangkalajan Rd, T053-920111, www.chiangmaioasis.com. Luxurious day spa in the old city offering different treatment packages varying from 1 to 4 hrs.

Tao Garden Health Resort, 274 Moo 7, Luang Nua Doi Saket, T053-921200, www.tao-garden.com. Situated 30 mins outside Chiang Mai, Tao Garden is an expensive alcohol- and smoke-free retreat. Treatments begin with a Chinese medical check-up, after which you can access many different types of massages, detox methods and aromatherapies, such as holistic dental treatment, inner smile meditation, colonic therapy and a blood-cleaner zapper.

Massage courses For those who want to find out more about Thai massage, a number of courses are available.

OMH Thai Massage School, Old Chiang Mai Medical Hospital, 238/8 Wuolai Rd (opposite Old Chiang Mai Cultural Centre, Chiang Mai-Hod Rd), T053-275085, www.thaimassageschool.ac.th. Offers a choice of courses ranging from 7 to 30 hrs.

Thai Massage School of Chiang Mai, 203/6 Mae Jo Rd, T053-854330, www.tmcschool.com. Fully accredited by the Thai Department of Education, TMC offers courses from foundation to advanced level, including an intensive 5-week curriculum.

Tour operators

See also Trekking, below. Many of the larger tour companies and travel agents also arrange visas and tours to Burma and Vietnam. Going rates are: Burma, ฿5000 (30 days); Vietnam, ฿2600 (30 days). Visas take 3-7 days. Visas on arrival when travelling to Laos or Cambodia.

A range of day tours run from Chiang Mai. Prices seem to vary between companies; examples of day tours include: Wat Phrathat Doi Suthep, the Phu Ping Palace and a Meo village (฿1000); the Mae Sa Valley to visit a waterfall, orchid farm and elephants at work (฿1000); Doi Inthanon National Park (฿1200-1400); Bor Sang (the Umbrella village) and San Kamphaeng (฿300); Chiang Rai and the Golden Triangle (฿1500-1800).

Make sure you know exactly what is included in the price; some travellers have complained of hidden costs, such as road tolls, tips for guides, entrance fees, etc. It is advisable to shop around to secure the best deal. Most tour operators are concentrated around Tha Phae Gate, Chang Klang and Moon Muang (in the vicinity of Tha Phae Gate), so this process is not as time-consuming as it may seem. Most operators will also book air, train and bus tickets out of Chiang Mai. The **TAT** recommends that services should only be

Trekking around Chiang Mai

There are scores of trekking companies in Chiang Mai and hundreds of places selling trekking tours. Competition is stiff and most companies provide roughly the same assortment of treks, ranging from one night to over a week. Not many places actually organize the trek themselves and it is rare to meet the guide – or other people in the group – before leaving for the trek. The quality of the guide rather than the organizing company usually makes the trip successful or not and the happiest trekkers are often those who have done their homework and found a company with long-term, permanent staff who they can meet beforehand.

For further information, see Tour operators, page 55.

Like many other areas of tourism, trekking is suffering from its own success. Companies organizing treks are finding it increasingly difficult to present their products as authentic get-away-from-it-all adventures when there is such a high probability of bumping into another group of tourists. As numbers increase so travellers are demanding more authenticity in their trekking experiences. The answer is to avoid the environs of Chiang Mai and trek in less pressured areas like Mae Hong Son, Nan and Pai. Many trek operators – like those along Moon Muang Road – are advertising special non-tourist routes, although these so-called special routes are virtually indistinguishable from established routes. Some companies even claim to offer a money-back guarantee should they come into contact with other trekkers.

The TAT office distributes a list of recommended trekking operators and a leaflet on what to look out for when choosing your trip. The Tribal Research Institute (see page 31), situated at the back of the Chiang Mai University campus on Huay Kaew Road, provides information on the various hilltribes, maps of the trekking areas, and a library of books on these fascinating people. You can also download a useful pdf file from their website, www.chmai.com/tribal/content.html.

When to trek The best time to trek is during the cool, dry season between October and February. In March and April, although it is dry, temperatures can be high and the vegetation is parched. During the wet season, paths are muddy and walking can be difficult.

What to take Trekkers who leave their cards for safekeeping in their guesthouses have sometimes found that a large bill awaits them on their return. A safety desposit box hired at a bank is the safest way to leave your valuables ((banks on Tha Phae Road have safety deposits and charge about ฿200 per month).

Trekking companies should advise on what to take and many provide rucksacks, bought from companies that register with the Tourist Business and Guide Registration Office. It provides a list of all such companies. Standards can vary between tours (and guides) within tour companies, and these standards can change rapidly, so word of mouth is often the best guarantee of a good experience.

Buffalo Tours, 145/1 Rachadamnoen Rd, Phrasinjuha, Muang, T53-284594. Arrange tours throughout the region. Also has offices in Bangkok and Phuket.

Untouched Thailand, T08-4614 4078 (mob), www.untouchedthailand.com. Clued-up Thai-run outfit offering half- and 1-day tours around Chiang Mai, plus longer trips further afield.

sleeping bags, first-aid kits and food. However, the following is a checklist of items that might be useful: good walking shoes; bed sheet (blanket/sleeping bag in the cold season November-February); waterproof (July-October); insect repellent; toiletries (soap, toothpaste, toilet papre); small first-aid kit (including antiseptic, plasters, diarrhoea pills, salt tablets); sun protection (suncream/sun hat); photocopy of passport (if venturing into border area); and water bottle (to cut down on the plastic bottles accumulating in the hills in the north). Remember to take protection against mosquitoes; long trousers and long-sleeved shirts are essential for the night-time.

Choosing a trekking company When choosing a guide for the trip, ensure that he or she can speak the hilltribe dialect as well as good English (or French, German etc). Guides must hold a 'Professional Guide Licence'. Treks must be registered with the Tourist Police; to do this the guide must supply the Tourist Police with a photocopy of the Identity page of your passport and your date of entry stamp. You can check on a company's reputation by contacting the police department. Note that the best guides may move between companies or work for more than one.

Health precautions By living in hilltribe villages, even if only for a few days, the health hazard is amplified significantly. Inoculation against hepatitis and protection against malaria are both strongly recommended. Particular dietary care should be exercised: do not drink unboiled or untreated water and avoid uncooked vegetables. Although the hilltribe population may look healthy, remember that the incidence of parasitic infection in most communities is not far off 100%.

Costs It does not take long to work out the going price for a trek – just ask around. For a basic walking trek, costs are ฿250-500 per day, the cheaper end of the the range relating to trekking companies that specialize in the backpacking market; if rafting and elephant rides are also included, the cost rises to ฿500-1000 per day. Many trekking companies and some guesthouses take donations to help support the hill people, and in particular the many thousands of displaced refugees from Burma.

Opium smoking For some, one of the attractions of trekking is the chance to smoke opium. It should be remembered that opium smoking, as well as opium cultivation, is illegal in Thailand. It is also not unusual for first-time users to experience adverse physical and psychological side effects. Police regularly stop and search tourists who are motorcycle trekking. Be careful not to carry any illicit substances.

Trekking companies

The city's **TAT office**, 105/1 Chiang Mai-Lamphun Rd, T053-248604, has information on trekking in the region, including a list of licensed agencies. Many of the companies are concentrated on Tha Phae, Chaiyaphum, Moon Muang and Kotchasan roads. Standards change so rapidly that recommending companies is a dangerous business, but the safest bet is to find somewhere with permanent, long-term staff. One such outfit is **Panda Tour**, 127/5 Rajchapakinai Rd, T053-418 920, www.pandatourchiangmai.com.

Prices for treks are highly variable with 2-day trips costing somewhere between ฿2000-3000; 3-day treks ฿2500-4000 and 4-day treks ฿3000-5000. Be aware that the better trips usually cost more, either because they're more off the beaten track and therefore further away, or because the company is paying for one of the better guides, who are worth their weight in gold. If you find a trek for a price that seems too good to be true, it probably is, and will end up being a waste of both money and time.

Zip lining
Flight of the Gibbons, T053-010660, www.treetopasia.com. At over ฿3000 a head, this isn't the cheapest activity, but it is certainly one of the most fun. Fly from tree top to tree top in the jungle just outside Chiang Mai along 5 km of zip lines. Adrenalin fix guaranteed.

Lampang *p34*
Massage
Northern Herbal Medicine Society, opposite Wat Prakaew Don Tao. Traditional Thai massage – good value at ฿150 per hr, 108 herbs available for the full treatment.

⊖ Transport

Chiang Mai *p20, maps p22 and p26*
Air
Chiang Mai airport, 3 km southwest of town, T053-270222, www.chiangmai airportonline.com, is now a very busy and important international hub. At the time of writing numerous airlines – THAI, AirAsia, Nok Air, Kan Air, Bangkok Airways and Korean Air – connect Chiang Mai with various domestic and regional destinations, including **Bangkok**, **Phuket**, **Pai**, **Mae Hong Son**, **Kuala Lumpur**, **Sukhothai** and **Seoul**. Air Bagan fly to **Yangon** (Burma); SilkAir flies to **Singapore**; Korean Air flies to **Seoul**; Lao Airlines fly to **Vientiane** and **Luang Prabang**. Nok Air also flies to several domestic destinations in the north: **Mae Hong Son**, **Mae Sot**, **Nan** and **Udon Thani**, as does Kan Air: **Pai**, **Nan**, **Mae Hong Son** and **Phitsanulok**. Be aware that routes on budget airlines can change quickly and you should check at the time of travel.
  Airline offices Air Bagan, 166/12 Changklan Rd, T053-284985. THAI, 240

Prapokkloa Rd, in the Old City, T053-920921. **AirAsia**, 416 Tha Phae Rd (next to Starbucks, Tha Phae Gate). **Bangkok Airways**, Chiang Mai International Airport, T053-281519 ext 11-14. **Nok Air**, Chiang Mai International Airport, T053-922183.

Bus
The long-distance Arcade Bus Station is northeast of town by the Superhighway, and most companies will provide a transfer service: pick-up points are Anusarn Market, Narawat Bridge, Sang Tawan Cinema and Chiang Inn Hotel Lane. There is an information desk within the main terminal building, with information on all departure times and prices. The tourist police also have a desk here. Regular connections with **Bangkok**'s Northern bus terminal (10 hrs), **Phitsanulok** (6 hrs), **Mae Sai** (5 hrs), **Sukhothai** (5 hrs), **Chiang Rai** (3-4 hrs, see below), **Mae Sariang** (4-5 hrs), **Mae Hong Son** (5-7 hrs), **Pai** (3-5 hrs), **Nan** (6 hrs) and other northern towns. In early 2012 a new route was opened linking Chiang Mai with Luang Prabang in Laos (18 hrs). A number of tour companies organize coaches to Bangkok; these are concentrated in the Anusarn Market area and usually provide transport to the Arcade terminal, from where the buses depart.
  Buses to closer destinations (such as **Mae Rim**, **Phrao**, **Chiang Dao**, **Fang**, **Tha Ton** and **Lamphun**) go from Chang Phuak Bus Station, 127/28 Chang Phuak Rd, north of Chang Puak Gate, T053-211586. For **Pasang**, there are direct buses from the Arcade Bus Station, or catch a bus to Lamphun and then a connecting bus to Pasang. For **Bor Sang** and **San Kamphaeng**, take a red bus running along the north side of Charoen Muang Rd, opposite the San Pa Khoi Market east of the Narawat Bridge, or take a bus from Chiang Puak Gate.
  To **Chiang Rai**, buses taking the *sai kao* (old route) leave from the Old Lamphun Rd, near the Narawat Bridge; those on the *sai mai* (new route) leave from the Arcade bus station.

Motorbiking in Northern Thailand

Renting a motorbike to explore Thailand's north is fast becoming one of the most popular ways to tour this part of the kingdom. Bike rental and fuel is relatively cheap, with everything from 50cc automatic mopeds through to giant 1200cc BMWs on offer in Chiang Mai.

If you plan to ride a bike then your first port of call should be the Golden Triangle Rider's website and forum, www.gt-rider.com. Put together by David Unkovich, an Australian expat with over 25 years' experience of riding in northern Thailand, you'll find everything you need right down to road surfaces, suggestions for the best food and accommodation, reviews of Chiang Mai's different rental outlets and even safety tips. Unkovich also produces a set of essential maps that cover the north of Thailand in great detail and include some off-road trails. These maps are on sale in many outlets in Chiang Mai – the more expensive laminated one is almost indestructible.

"If you have a week, the best route is to head for the far north," says Unkovich. "Head north from Chiang Mai to Doi Ang Khang, a mountain-top high above the Burmese border, before carrying on up to Tha Ton and Mae Salong. Pass through Doi Tung towards Mae Sai, through the Golden Triangle and along the Mekong to Chiang Khong. Nearby is Phu Chi Fah, where a dramatic mountain road edges along the Laos border. From there swing south to Nan on the 1148 – bikers' paradise – and from Nan it's a few hours back to Chiang Mai. Just rent a bike and get on with it. You won't need a guide."

The old route goes via Lampang and Phayao (6 hrs); the new route takes Rte 1019, via Doi Saket and Wiang Papao hot springs (4 hrs).

Car or jeep hire

Rates start at ฿800-1800 per day, ฿6000 per week. Many guesthouses will arrange rental, or there are outfits along Chaiyaphum and Moon Muang roads. **Avis** and **Thai Rent A Car** have booths at the airport. **North Wheels**, 70/4-8 Chaiyaphum Rd, T053-874478, www.northwheels.com. Long-established local operator with competitive rates.

Motorbike hire

The wearing of helmets in Chiang Mai city is compulsory. Enforcement of this is fairly lax, but prepare for a ฿300 fine if you are caught.

Motorbike hire is available along Chaiyuphum Rd, Moon Muang Rd, Loi Kroa Rd and at many guesthouses. Rates start at about ฿200 for a 125 cc Honda Dream and rise up to ฿1000 for a chopper or sports bike. Insurance is not available for small bikes and most policies only protect you from 50% of the repair costs.

Mae Ping Car Rent & Travel, 99/4 Loi Kroa Rd, T053-273-975, T08-1595 3351. Scooter, motorbike and car hire.

POP, 51 Kotchasan Rd, T053-276014, ฿250 for 24 hrs.

Songthaews/tuk-tuks

As the municipal bus service is almost non-existent, red *songthaews* (pick-up trucks with 2 rows of seating in the rear) are the most common way to get around town. Rather than follow a fixed route, they roam the main streets looking for passengers. If they're heading in your direction they'll drop you off, usually for ฿20 per person, sometimes ฿30-40 if your destination is further afield. Tuk-tuks charge a minimum ฿40 per trip, ฿80-120 for longer journeys.

Train

Flights with the low-cost airlines often work out only slightly more expensive – and much quicker – but travelling to and from Chiang Mai by train is still the most scenic option. The station is in the east of the town, on Charoen Muang Rd, across the Ping River. Ticket office is open 0500-2100. Information, T053-244795; reservations T053-242094 or www.railway.co.th. Left luggage service available. Regular connections with **Bangkok**'s Hualamphong station and towns along the route (11-15 hrs). There are both day-time and sleeper services; booking is required for both.

Lampang *p34*
Air

Daily flights to **Bangkok** via **Phitsanulok** with Bangkok Air.

Airline offices Bangkok Airways, Lampang Airport, 175 Sanambin Rd, T054-821522.

Bus

It is possible to leave luggage at the information counter in the terminal. Regular connections with **Bangkok**'s Northern bus terminal (9 hrs), **Chiang Mai** (2 hrs), **Chiang Rai**, **Sukhothai**, **Tak** and **Phitsanulok**. Buses from Chiang Mai leave from the Old Chiang Mai–Lamphun Rd, near the tourist office. Buses also go east to **Phrae** (2½ hrs) and on to **Nan**; these leave throughout the day, about 1 every hr.

Train

Regular connections with **Bangkok** (12 hrs) and **Chiang Mai** (2 hrs).

ⓘ Directory

Chiang Mai *p20, maps p22 and p26*
Emergencies T191. **Immigration office** Fang Rd, 300 m before the entrance to the airport, T053-201755, www.chiangmaiimm.com, Mon-Fri 0830-1200, 1300-1630 (visa extensions possible, see page 17). **Medical services** Chiang Mai's medical services have a good reputation. The most popular expat hospital is **Ram**, where there is 24-hr service available and good English-speaking doctors. Chiang Mai Ram Hospital, Boonruangrit Rd, T053-920300. McCormick Hospital, Kaew Nawarat Rd, T053-921777, **Malaria Centre**, Boonruangrit Rd, north of Suan Dok Gate. **Dentist** Ram Hospital has a good dental clinic. **Police** Corner of Phra Singh and Jhaban roads. **Tourist Police**: in the same building as the TAT office on the Chiang Mai-Lamphun Rd, at the Arcade Bus Station, the night market and at the airport.

Lampang *p34*
Medical services Khelang Nakom Hospital, Phahonyothin Rd, T054-225100.

Western loop: Pai, Mae Hong Son, Mae Sariang

Some of the most spectacular scenery in Thailand lies to the west of Chiang Mai, where the Tenasserim range divides Burma from Thailand. Travelling northwest from Chiang Mai on Route 107, then Route 108, the road passes through the Mae Sa Valley to the popular backpacker and trekking town of Pai, a distance of 140 km. From Pai to Soppong is more stunning scenery, then onto the hill town of Mae Hong Son, a centre for trekking and home to fine Burmese-style wats. Due south to Mae Sariang (160 km from Mae Hong Son), close to the Burmese border, there is some more excellent trekking, then the road follows narrow river valleys to Doi Inthanon, one of the country's most famous peaks and national parks.

Pai → *For listings, see pages 66–73.*

The road from Chiang Mai winds its way through scintillating landscapes and thick forest until the view unfolds into a broad valley. In the middle, encircled by handsome, high ridges, sits Pai. Over the last 25 years this small mountain village has transformed itself into one of Northern Thailand's most popular destinations. These days, with its organic eateries and reggae bars Pai could be considered a travellers' oasis. Even hip young city dwellers from Bangkok are catching onto the area's beauty, facilities, hot springs and diversity – Lisu, Karen, Shan, Red Lahu, Kuomintang-Chinese are all represented.

Pai offers excellent trekking, superb rafting, a plethora of places to get massaged and pummelled, some great food and the town still manages to retain a sense of charm. The range of accommodation is also huge – everything from boutique spa resorts through to cheap and nasty huts populated with wasted travellers. All this makes Pai seductive to the visitor who likes to consume their experience rather create it. Don't come here thinking you're going to get an authentic slice of Thai life. This is a generic, contrived Khaosan Road-style experience, though, admittedly, in very pleasant surroundings. Helping to cement Pai's growing status, an airstrip has opened just to the north of town with a couple of flights a day linking Pai with Chiang Mai.

There are two markets in town – the *talaat sot* (fresh market) on Rangsiyanon Road and the *talaat saeng thong araam* on Khetkelang Road. The finest monastery in town is Thai Yai-style **Wat Klang** near the bus station. There's another monastery, **Wat Phrathat Mae Yen**, about 1.5 km east of town, on a hill. Head a further 3 km east and you'll arrive at Pai's famous **hot springs**. The sulphurous water bubbles up through a systems of streams – bring a towel and jump in. There's also a campsite here.

Lisu, **Shan**, **Red Lahu** and **Kuomintang-Chinese villages** are all in the vicinity. Most guesthouses provide rough maps detailing hilltribe villages, hot springs, caves, waterfalls and other sights. For further information on hilltribes and trekking, see boxes, pages 30 and 56. For activities such as rafting, elephant safaris, cookery and aromatherapy classes, see What to do, page 71.

Soppong → *For listings, see pages 66-73.*

Soppong, or Phang Ma Pha, is a small way station between Pai and Mae Hong Son. It is slowly metamorphosing into an alternative to Pai – there's no real backpacker 'scene' here, though there a few great guesthouses offering a decent array of trekking services. Many people come here to trek and explore the surrounding countryside. Most of the guesthouses organize treks and this is one of the best bases hereabouts. Local villages include Lisu, Black and Red Lahu, and Shan. This is also a good place to escape to if what you want to do is nothing. The journey from Pai to Soppong is stunning with magnificent views. The road winds through beautiful cultivated valleys and forest.

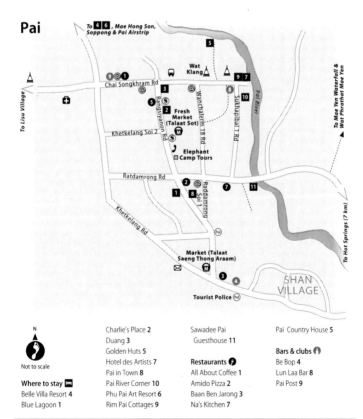

Pai

N Not to scale

Where to stay 🛏
Belle Villa Resort **4**
Blue Lagoon **1**
Charlie's Place **2**
Duang **3**
Golden Huts **5**
Hotel des Artists **7**
Pai in Town **8**
Pai River Corner **10**
Phu Pai Art Resort **6**
Rim Pai Cottages **9**
Sawadee Pai
Guesthouse **11**

Restaurants 🍴
All About Coffee **1**
Amido Pizza **2**
Baan Ben Jarong **3**
Na's Kitchen **7**
Pai Country House **5**

Bars & clubs 🍸
Be Bop **4**
Lun Laa Bar **8**
Pai Post **9**

Around Soppong

Guesthouses provide maps of the surrounding countryside and villages, with tracks marked. The main sight is **Lod Cave (Tham Lod)** ① *0800-1700*, about 10 km from town. The cave (in fact a series of three accessible caves) has been used for habitation since prehistoric times and is a small part of what is presumed to be one of the largest cave systems in northern Thailand. To explore the accessible areas of the cave system takes around two hours; guides hire out their services – and their lamps – to take visitors through the cave, which has a large stream running through it. Rafts are available to traverse the stream. In the nearby village you'll find **Cave Lodge** (see page 68), an excellent guesthouse, which offers trips through the caves and serves great coffee and food.

Mae Lanna is a quiet, highland Shan village/town 16 km northwest of Soppong, off Route 1095. The area offers limestone caves, good forest walks and stunning limestone scenery. To get there, take a bus towards Mae Hong Song and get off at the turn-off for Mae Lanna, about 10 km west of Soppong. Pick-ups run the steep 6 km up to the village – or walk. Guesthouses in Soppong provide sketch maps of the area, with hiking trails marked.

Mae Hong Son → *For listings, see pages 66-73.*

Mae Hong Son lies in a forested valley, surrounded by soaring verdant hills and just about lives up to its claim of being the 'Switzerland of Thailand'. The road from Pai is continuous switchback, cutting through spectacular scenery and communities of diverse ethnicities. On a clear day, the short flight from Chiang Mai is breathtaking – the plane crosses a range of high hills before spiralling down into a tight series of continuous banks, depositing its passengers almost in the middle of the town.

An excellent centre for trekking, the town is changing rapidly (some would say has changed) from a backpackers' hideaway to a tour centre, with the construction of two major hotels and a proliferation of 'resort'-style hotels. Despite this, Mae Hong Son still manages to retain peaceful, upland vibe.

Arriving in Mae Hong Son

Getting there and around There are regular flights from Chiang Mai. You can easily walk from the airport to the town. The airport is to the north of town on Niveshpishan Road. It has an information counter and currency exchange booth, and *songthaews* are also available for hire. The bus station is at the northern end of town on Khunlum Praphat Road; there are plenty of connections with Chiang Mai, other destinations in this area of western Thailand and Bangkok's Northern bus terminal. It's a short walk to town and most guesthouses from the bus station. Mae Hong Son is small enough to walk around and tuk-tuk journeys around town cost ฿10-20. It is a friendly, accessible and amenable place. ➤➤ *See Transport, page 73, for further information.*

Best time to visit During the cool season (December to February), when the days are warm and clear and the nights are fresh, you'll need a sweater as evening temperatures can get as low as 2°C.

Tourist information TAT, 4 Ratchathumpitak Rd, T053-612982, www.tourismthailand.org/maehongson, provides leaflets and information.

Background

Mae Hong Son Province is about as far removed from 'Thailand' as you are likely to get, with only an estimated 2% of the population here being ethnic Thais. The great majority belong to one of the various hilltribes: mostly Karen, but also Lisu, Hmong and Lahu.

Mae Hong Son has always been caught between the competing powers of Burma and Siam/Thailand. For much of recent history the area has been under the (loose) control of various Burmese kingdoms. The influence of Burmese culture is also clearly reflected in the architecture of the town's many monasteries.

Mae Hong Son

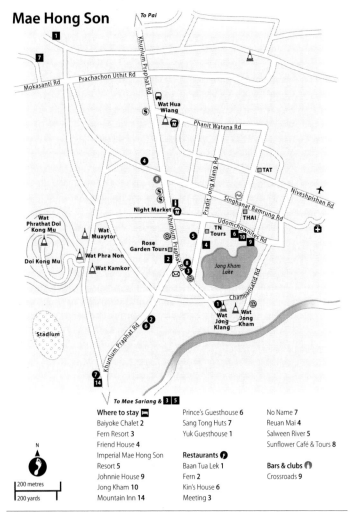

Where to stay 🛏
Baiyoke Chalet **2**
Fern Resort **3**
Friend House **4**
Imperial Mae Hong Son
Resort **5**
Johnnie House **9**
Jong Kham **10**
Mountain Inn **14**

Prince's Guesthouse **6**
Sang Tong Huts **7**
Yuk Guesthouse **1**

Restaurants 🍴
Baan Tua Lek **1**
Fern **2**
Kin's House **6**
Meeting **3**

No Name **7**
Reuan Mai **4**
Salween River **5**
Sunflower Café & Tours **8**

Bars & clubs 🍸
Crossroads **9**

N

| 200 metres
| 200 yards

Mae Hong Son also has a murky reputation for illegal logging; this area has some of the richest forests in the country. At the beginning of 1998, revelations surfaced about an alleged massive bribe to officials of the Royal Forestry Department, to overlook logging in the Salween conservation area.

Places in Mae Hong Son

Most postcards of the town picture the lake, with **Wat Jong Klang**, a Burmese wat, in the background. It is particularly beautiful in the early morning, when mist rises off the lake. Wat Jong Klang started life as a rest pavilion for monks on pilgrimage, with a wat being built by the Shans living in the area between 1867 and 1871. The monastery contains some 50 carved Burmese *tukata* (wooden dolls) depicting characters from the Jataka stories, as well as a series of mediocre painted glass panels. In the same compound is **Wat Jong Kham**, which contains a large seated Buddha. **Wat Hua Wiang**, next to the market, contains an important Burmese-style brass Buddha image – the Phra Chao Phla La Khaeng. It is said that the image was cast in nine pieces in Burma and brought to Mae Hong Son along the Pai River.

Doi Kong Mu, the hill overlooking the town, provides superb views of the valley and is home to the Burmese-style **Wat Phrathat Doi Kong Mu**, constructed by the first King of Mae Hong Son in the mid-19th century. At the foot of Doi Kung Mu Hill is **Wat Phra Non**, which contains a 12-m-long Burmese-style reclining Buddha. The main fresh **market** in town is on Phanit Watana Road, next to Wat Hua Wiang. The usual commodities from slippery catfish to synthetic clothing are sold here, together with some produce from Burma. ► *For tours and trekking see page 72.*

Around Mae Hong Son → For listings, see pages 66-73.

Mae Aw, officially known in Thailand as Ban Rak Thai, is a Hmong and KMT (Kuomintang the remnants of Chiang Kai Shek's army) village in the mountains, 22 km north of Mae Hong Son, on the border with Burma. (Chiang Kai Shek was the Chinese Republican leader who fought the Communists and then fled to Taiwan when the latter were victorious. Remnants of his army and supporters also took refuge in Thailand.) There are stunning views over Burma and the trip here is worthwhile in itself. From Mae Hong Son, take a *songthaew* (two hours) from Singhanat Bamrung Road (at about 0800), or arrange a trek.

Tham Plaa (Fish Cave), 16 km northeast of town off Route 1095, is another worthwhile excursion, which can be combined with a trip to Mae Aw. The name of the cave refers to the numbers of carp that live in the cave pools – several hundred, some exceeding 1 m in length. The carp are believed to be sacred. From the gate, a path leads across a river to the cave.

Khun Yuam and Muang Pon

ⓘ *Buses plying the Mae Hong Son to Mae Sariang road will pass through both towns – Khun Yuam is about 90 mins south of Mae Hong Son, Maung Pon is 15 mins further. Homestays at Muang Pon can arrange pick-ups from Khun Yuam, Mae Hong Son and Mae Sariang.*

Roughly halfway between Mae Sariang and Mae Hong Son is the bustling market town of Khun Yuam. The town itself has few attractions yet it is an engaging and friendly place to stop off for a couple of days if you want to make a slow meander through this part of the country. Most of the people who live here are Karen, Shan or Hmong. There is a pretty Hmong/Burmese-style temple 5 km to the west at **Wat To Phae**, which is worth a look; it houses a 150-year-old tapestry just to the side of the main altar. There is also a **War Museum** ⓘ *on the main road near the town centre, Tue-Sat 0930-1200, 1400-1600, ฿90,* which focuses on the plight of Japanese soldiers during World War Two. Thousands died here as Khun Yuam was home to a Japanese army hospital. The museum houses a collection of poignant artefacts left behind by the dying soldiers.

The nearby Shan village of Muang Pon, about 15 km to the south of Khun Yuam on the road to Mae Sariang, hosts an excellent homestay programme that is run, managed and owned by local people. Stay here for a few days and you'll get a chance to engage in a genuine encounter with local people a million miles from the usual intrusions of a 'hilltribe' trek. Nearby you'll find hot springs, mountain walks and a small hilltop temple.

Mae Sariang → *For listings, see pages 66-73.*

The capital of Amphoe district, Mae Sariang is a small market town on the banks of the Yuam River, and a good departure point for trekking. The road from Chom Thong runs up the Ping Valley, before turning west to follow the Chaem River, climbing steadily through beautiful dipterocarp forest, the Op Luang National Park (17 km from Hod), and into the mountains of western Thailand. There is little to draw people here, except as a stopping-off point for Mae Hong Son or as a starting point for trekking. The town is small and leafy, with many of the houses still built of wood – a comparative oasis after the dusty urban centres. The bus station is on Mae Sariang Road in the centre of town, five minutes' walk from the Riverside Guesthouse, next to Wat Jong Sung.

There are a handful of unremarkable wats. Wat Utthayarom, known locally as Wat Chom Soong, is Burmese in style but also displays two Mon-inspired white *chedis*. Other monasteries include Wat Sri Bunruang (in town) and Wat Joom Thong (on a hill, overlooking town). The latter has a large and recently constructed white seated Buddha image surveying the valley below. The town also has a better stock of wooden shophouses than most Thai towns – that is on Laeng Phanit Road (the river road). The morning market operates from a plot on Sathit Phon Road and there is also an evening market – good for stall food – at the end of Wiang Mai Road.

Trekking, rafting, cave and waterfall visits and elephants rides are also possible, see What to do, page 72.

Western loop: Pai, Mae Hong Son and Mae Sariang listings

For hotel and restaurant price codes and other relevant information, see pages 8-12.

🛏 Where to stay

Pai *p61, map p62*
There is no shortage of places to stay in and around Pai, though it is advisable to book ahead during high season and big festivals as rooms in town can run out fast. Recent years have seen the emergence of more expensive and mid-range options in and around the town. If you want to stay out of town, there are plenty of good, cheap

options east of the river. The selection here is a cross section of what's available.
$$$$ Belle Villa Resort, 113 Moo 6, T053-698226, www.bellevillaresort.com. Thai country-style wooden cottages or modern rooms in a concrete wing. A bit out of town but has a pretty riverside location, plus a swimming pool.
$$$$ Hotel des Artists, 99 Moo 3, Chai Songkhram Rd, T053-699539, www.hotel artists.com. Just across the road is this attractive boutique hotel. A renovated Thai noble house, the hotel has plenty of character and the rooms are comfortable

and clean with good facilities. The four Riverview Suite rooms offer beautiful views. Prices come down significantly outside high season. Recommended.

$$$$ Pai River Corner, Chai Shongkhram Rd, T053-699049, www.pairivercorner.com. Gorgeous little resort laid out beside the river around a nicely kept garden of mini-villas. All are a/c, with en suite hot showers and balconies. Stylish and well kept, the upper rooms come complete with big, breezy balconies. There's also a small pool here. Recommended.

$$$ Phu Pai Art Resort, 5 km north of town, T053-065111, www.phupai.com. Beautiful resort in a gorgeous location. Rooms are huge, with all the modern facilities you'd expect. Service is a bit patchy, but it's still good value.

$$$ Rim Pai Cottage, 3 Chai Songkhram Rd, T053-699133, www.rimpaicottage.com. Good position on the river and a nice choice of huts.

$$ Blue Lagoon, 227 Moo 4 Pai (on main road in centre of town), T053-699998, www.paibluelagoon.com. Well-run and priced. Clean, decent rooms, excellent disabled facilities. Pool.

$$ Pai In Town, Rangsiyanon Rd, T053-699085, www.paiintown.com. A little soulless, but a modern, clean and reasonably priced option right in the heart of town. Within easy reach of restaurants, bars and shopping. Free Wi-Fi.

$$ Sawadi Pai Guesthouse, Ratdamrong Rd, T084-648 4829. Offers comfortable, modern bungalows in a good location by the river. A/c, TV and free Wi-Fi in all rooms. Good value for the location.

$ Charlie's Place, Rangsiyanon Rd, T053-699039. One of the larger places in town, with a range of accommodation from dormitory beds to more expensive and less run-down brick bungalows with attached bathrooms, all set in a largish garden. Good trekking organized from here.

$ Duang, 5 Rangsiyanon Rd, T053-699101. Clean, friendly English-speaking and

family-run guesthouse; it's opposite the bus station, so noisy at night. A choice of rooms to suit all budgets, good restaurant (excellent coffee and French bread), trekking organized.

$ Golden Huts, 107 Moo 3 Wiang Tai, T053-699949. Very quiet, beautiful out-of-the-way location on the riverbank. Quiet and relaxing atmosphere, French owner provides a friendly service. Small but adequate restaurant with good food and great views. Good budget option. Recommended.

Soppong *p62*

$$$ Baan Cafe Resort, next to main road, T053-617081. Nicely laid-out rooms and bungalows, some with terraces overlooking a river, which can be used to bathe in. Pleasant gardens, friendly, good food. Small shop selling local produce. Recommended.

$$$ Little Eden, on main road, T053-617054, www.littleeden-guesthouse.com. Wide selection of A-frame bungalows and a river-view house. Rooms are fresh and well-kept, a/c, hot water and en suite available. Attractive gardens, restaurant and swimming pool. Recommended.

$$ The Rock Garden Resort, 1 km from the village towards Mae Hong Son, T053-617134, www.therockresort.com. Reasonably priced bungalows and houses in overlooking the river in a beautiful garden setting. Houses available for up to 7 people. Good restaurant and rafting tours organized. Recommended.

$$ Soppong River Inn, 500 m from village centre towards Mae Hong Son, T053-617107, www.soppong.com. Range of great huts, some with verandas, overlooking a small gorge. Also offers trekking service, massage and fresh coffee. Friendly and recommended.

$ Kemarin Garden, a short way down a lane 200 m up the hill towards Pai. 4 simple A-frame bungalows, peaceful rural position with views over the hills, clean hot-water showers. Friendly management (but no English spoken). Recommended.

Around Soppong p63

There are several places to stay in Mae Lanna.

$$-$ Cave Lodge, T053-617203, www.cave lodge.com. Cave Lodge is a labour of love for its Aussie owner, John Spies. A cluster of small bungalows cling to a steep rock face, which leads down to a small glade and stream. Facilities are basic but include everything from en suite rooms with hot water to dorms, and even a home-made sauna. Excellent Western, Thai and local cuisine available. The owner has an incredible local knowledge of the nearby cave systems, trekking routes and different ethnic groups. From Soppong, a motorbike taxi costs ฿70, or walk the 6.5 km from the villlage. One of the best guesthouses in the country, attracting a real cross-section of travellers. Highly recommended.

Mae Hong Son p63, map p64

$$$$ Mountain Inn, 112/2 Khunlum Praphat Rd, T053-611802, www.mhs mountaininn.com. A/c, well-thought-out rooms surround an atmospheric garden. Friendly management and also serves good food (see Restaurants, below).

$$$ Baiyoke Chalet Hotel, 90 Khunlum Praphat Rd, T053-613132, www.baiyoke mhs.com. Generic mid-range option in a good location at the heart of town. Clean, bright a/c rooms with decent facilities and free Wi-Fi. Rooms at the front of the hotel on the upper floors provide a good view of the lake.

$$$ Fern Resort, 2 km from Highway 108 at the turn-off for Ban Nua Hum Mae Sakut Village (5 km from town), Moo 10, T053-686110, www.fernresort.info. Wooden bungalows built on rice paddies in Shan style. Simple yet comfortable and tasteful. Set in lovely grounds, friendly and helpful staff; a good eco-friendly place, good local walks.

$$$ The Imperial Mae Hong Son Resort, 149 Moo 8, Pang Moo, T053-684444, www.imperialhotels.com. Beautiful accommodation located just south of town. Comfortable rooms with excellent views and great facilities. Swimming pool and a choice of restaurants.

$$ Sang Tong Huts, 250 Moo 11 T Pangmoo, T053-611680, www.sangtonghuts.com. Secluded spot northwest of town (near Yuk Guesthouse), with great views. Range of huts, dining area with great food and hilltribe coffee. Friendly and helpful owners. Recommended.

$ Friend House, 20 Pradit Jong Kham Rd, T053-620119. A teak house set back from the road. 10 very clean rooms (the shared showers are even cleaner), upstairs rooms have a view of the lake. Well managed and carefully maintained, small café downstairs for breakfast, laundry service. Recommended.

$ Johnnie House, 5/2 Udomchownites Rd, T053-611667. Peaceful position on the lakeside, 8 spotlessly clean and simple rooms, shared hot-water showers. Breakfast menu, laundry facilities. Friendly and quiet.

$ Jong Kham, 7 Udomchownites Rd, T053-611420. Lakeside, run-down bamboo bungalows with 'leaf' roofs and some cheaper rooms in the main house, largish garden, very popular.

$ Prince's Guesthouse, 31 Udomchaonitet Rd, T053-611136, princesguesthouse@ gmail.com. A/c and fan, some rooms overlooking the lake. Free Wi-Fi. Rooms are simple but clean. A good-value option in a good location. Recommended.

$ Yuk Guesthouse, 14 Sri Mongkol Rd, T053-611532. Tucked away behind a wat, this is a great place. Very clean and comfortable with a peaceful little garden. Small restaurant with good food. Free transport to and from the bus station and airport.

Khun Yuam and Muang Pon p65

$$ Ban Farang Guesthouse, 499 Moo 1 Khun Yuam Rd, www.banfarang-guest house.com, T053-622086. Decent, clean and friendly set of bungalows and rooms available here. Set just outside Khun Yuam town off the main road towards the north.

$ The Muang Pon Homestay, T053-684644, kunlaya_mall@hotmail.com. Several houses in this appealing Shan village take part in a very well-run homestay programme. You'll get treated as one of the family and introduced to the eccentricities of village life and earthy Shan cuisine. Rates includes breakfast and dinner. The villagers run excursions to nearby temples, villages, mountains and hot springs. Call or email to book and you'll be allocated your family. Transfers from Mae Hong Son and even Chiang Mai can be arranged for a set fee. This is one of the best examples of low-impact, fair trade tourism in Thailand. Highly recommended.

Mae Sariang p66

There are several reasonable guesthouses in Mae Sariang – most are 5-15 mins' walk from the bus station.
$$ Black Ant Coffee & Resort, 113/2 Laeng Phanit Rd, T053-682123, www.blackant coffee.net. Comfortable and attractive rooms in a balmy garden setting. Free breakfast, Wi-Fi and as much coffee as you can drink.
$$ River House Hotel, Laeng Phanit Rd (next to **Riverside**, see below), T053-683066, www.riverhousehotels.com. Clean and inviting rooms with great views from the balconies and good facilities. There is an excellent restaurant with riverside seating. The sister **River House Resort** nearby offers a slightly more expensive and luxurious option.
$$ Riverside, 85/1 Laeng Phanit Rd, T053-681188. A 5-min stroll from the bus station, this attractive building has large, clean rooms by the river and wonderful views from the breakfast/seating area. Remains a popular choice for travellers and is a good source of information. The owner has plans to expand across the river, building long-stay bungalows.
$ See View, 70 Wiang Mai Rd (across the river, and overlooking it, on the edge of town), T053-681556. Good-sized rooms in stone bungalows, smaller wooden rooms available, with shared facilities. Quiet and peaceful. It is a good source of information, the owner speaks English and is very helpful.

Pai p61, map p62

There are plenty of good eateries in town, ranging from local places offering duck noodle soup and *khao soi* (spicy northern noodles) to higher-end restaurants.
$$ Amido Pizza, Ratdamrong Rd. Awesome pizza, pasta and lasagne.
$$ Baan Ben Jarong, edge of town, on the way to Chiang Mai. High-class Thai cuisine – exceptional and one of the best places to eat in the area. Highly recommended.
$$ Pai River Corner, see Where to stay. Good food served in a pleasant riverside location. Lots of grills and BBQ, giant shrimp and steak. Decent Thai food as well. Breakfasts, coffees and lunches.
$ Na's Kitchen, Ratdamrong Rd. A favourite with expat locals, this small restaurant serves up tasty curries, Thai salads and other Thai dishes for bargain prices. Popular, so can be difficult to get a seat some evenings. Recommended.
$ Pai Country House, Rangsiyanon Rd. Open all day, this popular eatery, with a streetside eating area, offers an extensive menu of Western and Thai dishes. Good breakfasts, fresh coffee and refreshing shakes.

Bakeries
All About Coffee, Chai Songkhram Rd. An arty café, with huge open chicken and cashew sandwiches and a range of coffees and teas.

Foodstalls
There are plenty of stalls and street food venders, especially along the evening walking streets. Good pancakes and other food available.

Soppong p62
There are noodle stalls on the main road but if you want something more upmarket most of the guesthouses serve reasonable food. **Cave Lodge**, 6.5 km away (see Where to stay, above), makes a great lunch spot.

Mae Hong Son *p63, map p64*

The largest concentration of restaurants is on Khunlum Praphat Rd. The cheapest place to eat is in the night market. Some stalls by the lake offer mats to sit on right by the water – a perfect setting for an evening snack.

$$ Fern Restaurant, 87 Khunlum Praphat Rd. Large restaurant on road towards Mae Sariang. Smart, unpretentious and affordable, mostly Thai dishes including good frog, spicy salads and crispy fish, also ice cream.

$$ Mountain Inn, 112 Khunlum Praphat Rd (see Where to stay, above). Serves great Thai grub in its romantic garden.

$ Baan Tua Lek, Chamnansatid Rd, across from Jung Klang Temple, T053-620688. Coffee bar with cosy atmosphere, friendly staff and free Wi-Fi. A popular hangout. Coffee, smoothies and tea, as well as home-made sandwiches, cakes and cookies.

$ Kin's House, 89 Khunlum Praphat Rd (past **Fern Restaurant**). Selection of traditional and local Thai cuisine and Western food. Pleasant decor, café/bar atmosphere.

$ Meeting, Pradit Jong Klang Rd. Coffee and Internet downstairs and a restaurant upstairs offering reasonable Thai and Western fare. The views of the lake and temple from the upper limit make it an ideal spot for an evening meal or drink.

$ Restaurant (no name), next to **Mountain Inn**. Offers very authentic hilltribe dishes that are extremely popular with locals. The owner will let you taste before you buy.

$ Reuan Mai Restaurant, 5 Singhanat Bamrung Rd. Excellent restaurant in wooden house. Good atmosphere and choice of Thai and Western dishes. Specialities include deep-fried catfish and steaks, also serves breakfast. Recommended.

$ Salween River Restaurant, Pradit Jong Klang Rd, www.salweenriver.com. Top-notch budget fare at this small restaurant by the lake. Specializes in authentic Shan and Burmese dishes, but Western food also available. Recommended.

$ Sunflower Café and Tours, Pradit Jong Klang Rd, T053-620549, www.sunflower cafetour.com. Run by an Australian/Thai couple, popular with *farangs*. Good spot for breakfast and the best bread in town, good coffee, internet access, organizes tours and is a great source of information.

Bakeries

$ KK Bakery, near Pen Porn House. Fresh-baked cakes and bread, small selection of Thai dishes, set breakfasts, snacks and drinks.

Foodstalls

There's a market on Khunlum Praphat Rd and some stalls by the lake.

Khun Yuam and Muang Pon *p65*

Khun Yuam has a decent collection of rice and noodle shops and stalls on the main road towards the southern end of town. In Muang Pon the homestay progamme should meet most needs, though there are a few lunchtime noodle stalls and a bakery to be found in the village centre.

Mae Sariang *p66*

$$ Coriander in Redwood, Lang Phanit Rd. Excellent Thai fare and steaks in a beautiful wooden building. Friendly service, good menu and an attractive outside eating area too. Recommended.

$ River House Restaurant, Laeng Phanit Rd. Excellent range of food at reasonable prices in superb surroundings.

$ Ruan Phrae, down the *soi* to Wat Sri Bunruang, off Wiang Mai Rd. Thai and Chinese. Recommended.

Foodstalls

At the night market on Wiang Mai Rd (about 1 km from the centre of town).

🎵 Bars and clubs

Pai *p61, map p62*

Pai has no shortage of watering holes, whether you want to sip a quiet cocktail at sunset or dance until dawn. There are countless options in the town centre, with most closing up about midnight. There are a couple of outdoor bars east of the river that often go on all night.

Be Bop, Rangsiyanon Rd. Live music most nights, extremely popular with travellers. Great atmosphere, serves Western spirits.

Lun Laa Bar, Chai Songkhram Rd. Another popular venue with nightly live music. Great cocktails and foreign beers go down easily in a friendly and intimate atmosphere. Good deals on local beers.

Pai Post, Chai Songkhram Rd. Popular live music venue with live jazz and blues nightly. The musicians play out of an old Thai house, while a chilled and trendy crowd enjoy cocktails, wines and beers outside.

Mae Hong Son *p63, map p64*
There are a number of bar-restaurants by the lake that are perfect for an evening drink. Nightlife here is sedate compared to Pai, though there are a few Thai-style bars on the edge of town that stay open late.

Crossroads, at the crossroads of Sinahanat Bamrung Rd and Khunlum Praphat Rd. Drinks, limited bar menu and free pool upstairs.

⊛ Festivals

Pai *p61, map p62*
Late Jan Pai Reggae & Ska Music Festival, www.paifestival.com. Reggae fans and musicians come from all over the world for this 3-day festival. The event itself is held just out of town, but all of Pai is engulfed with reggae fever for this increasingly popular and sometimes raucous affair.

Mae Hong Son *p63, map p64*
Early Apr Poi Sang Long, young novices (10-16 years old) are ordained into the monkhood. Beforehand, they are dressed up as princes and, on the following day, there is a colourful procession through town starting from Wat Kham Ko.

⊙ Shopping

Pai *p61, map p62*
There are two **7-11s** in the centre of town and plenty of local shops. The central streets are closed to traffic at night and street traders sell everything from local handicrafts to popcorn.

Bookshops
Siam Books, 31 Chai Songkhram Rd. Best bookshop in town. Good selection of new and used English books. Limited selection of German, French and Swedish books.

Mae Hong Son *p63, map p64*
Plenty of **7-11s** and 2 good supermarkets, both near the crossroads in the town centre.

Bookshops
Asia Books, Khunlum Praphat Rd (next to Panorama Hotel). English-language novels and magazines.

Handicrafts
Several places on Singhanat Bamrung Rd.
Chokeadradet, 645 Khunlum Praphat Rd. For antiques, tribal handicrafts and junk. Recommended.
Thai Handicraft Centre, Khunlum Praphat Rd.

⊙ What to do

Pai *p61, map p62*
Rafting
Thai Adventure Rafting, just past the bus station, T053-699111, www.thairafting.com. The oldest whitewater rafting company in Thailand. It runs unforgettable, professional 2-day expeditions down the Pai River and beyond. It is run by Guy, a friendly Frenchman who has lived in Pai for 25 years. The river is only high enough Jul to end of Jan, trips start at ฿2500 and include everything from insurance to food/drinks. 1-day rafting trips cost ฿1500. It also offers 1-2 day treks and rock climbing expeditions.

There are other companies organizing similar (and cheaper) rafting trips in the area though none are as good.

Therapies
Traditional massage Opposite the **Rim Pai Cottages**, 68 Rachdamrong Rd, excellent massage (฿150-200 per hr) and friendly. Also available at several other places, including the **Foundation of Shivaga Kommapaj**.

Tour operators
There are a number of tour operators around town offering day trips, elephant riding and treks. Tour operators come and go, so be sure to ask around before booking. These are some of the more established, trusted outfits:
Duang Trekking (at Duang Guesthouse, see Where to stay). Basic trekking with all-inclusive prices of ฿1500-2500.
Thom Pai Elephant Camp Tours, 5/3 Rangsiyanon Rd, T053-699286. One of several companies offering elephant rides. Khun Thom, the owner, runs a professional set-up and treats her animals with respect. Her elephant camp is out of town towards the hot springs. Recommended – you can even swim with the elephants in the river or ride bareback.

Mae Hong Son *p63, map p64*
Therapies
Traditional massage and herbal steam bath is a Mae Hong Son speciality; particularly welcome for those just back from strenuous treks. There are plenty of places about town offering massage for about ฿150 per hr).

Tours operators
There are various day tours to sights such as Pha Sua Waterfall, Pang Tong Summer Palace, the KMT village of Mae Aw, Tham Plaa (Fish Cave) and Tham Nam Lot (Water Cave). A number of companies also advertise trips to the 'long-necked' Padaung, which involves a bumpy 1-hr trip to the 2 villages where they live. Many people deplore this type of tourism. Most guesthouses will organize

treks ranging from trips down the Salween River to the Burmese border to Mae Sot, elephant treks and rafting on the Pai River. The following operators are recommended:
Friend Tour at Friend Guesthouse, T053-620 119. Trekking, bamboo rafting, elephant rides, boat trips.
Rose Garden Tours, 86/4 Khunlum Prapaht Rd, T053-611577. Cultural and ecological tours. French also spoken.
Sunflower Tours, Sunflower Café. Eco-conscious birdwatching and nature treks.

Mae Sariang *p66*
Tour operators
Riverside (see Where to stay, page 69). Organizes treks through **Salawin Tours**. Treks include rafting, elephant rides, or visits to caves, waterfalls, Karen villages within the area or to the Burmese border.
Thailand Hilltribe Holidays, 66 Moo 12, Bankad Rd, T089-7009928, www.thailand hilltribeholidays.com. Organizes tours, treks and homestays in the region.
See View (see page 69). Organizes treks.

⊖ Transport

Pai *p61, map p62*
Air
There's a small airstrip just to the north of Pai. **Kan Airlines** run 1 daily flight each way (2 daily on weekends) in a tiny 12-seater Cessna between Pai and **Chiang Mai**. Tickets are available via their website, www.kanairlines.com, or their call centre (T025-516 111).

Bicycle
Mountain bike hire from ฿100 per day from the shop adjoining the **Duang**. **Pai Tai Bike Society**, opposite the bus station, which has information on routes and sights.

Bus
The bus stop is on Chai Songkhram Rd, near the centre of town. Buses leave hourly for Chiang Mai (3 hrs) and Mae Hong Son

(2 hrs) and cost ฿150. The last bus leaves town about 2 hrs before dusk. A few local slow buses leave for both destinations each day (about ฿70) but can take almost twice as long.

Motorbike
Hire costs ฿150-250 per day from several guesthouses and shops in town.

Soppong p62
Bus
There are 6-7 local buses each day (1 a/c) in each direction – west to **Mae Hong Son** (2 hrs), east to **Pai** (1 hr) and **Chiang Mai** (5 hrs). Minibuses pass through in each direction at least once an hour, but book ahead to be sure of a seat.

Motorbike/scooter
Most guesthouses can arrange hire, or try the shop close to the bus stop.

Mae Hong Son p63, map p64
Air
Regular daily connections on **Kan Airlines** (www.kanairlines.com) and **Nok Air** (www. nokair.com) with **Chiang Mai** (35 mins).

Bus
There are 2 routes to **Chiang Mai**: the northern, more gruelling route via Pai, or the route to the south, via Mae Sariang. Minibuses leave hourly in both directions every hr through the day (฿200) and take about 6 hrs. Slow buses are also available, but take much longer. Regular connections with **Bangkok**, 12½ hrs.

Car, motorbike and jeep
Many places hire out cars, jeeps, motorbikes and scooters. Prices for motorbikes/scooters from ฿150-250 per day (there are a couple of places at the southern end of Khunlum Praphat Rd), jeeps cost ฿800-1000 per day, while cars cost ฿1000-1200 per day.

Mountain bike
Mountain bikes are available for hire from 22 Singhanat Bamrun Rd, ฿100 per day.

Mae Sariang p66
Air
Kan Airlines (www.kanairlines.com) has 1 flight daily to **Chiang Mai**. The airport is located about 3 km from town on Laeng Phanit Rd.

Bus
7 buses daily to **Chiang Mai** and **Mae Hong Son** (both 4 hrs). There are also regular a/c minibus connections every day. Several a/c and non-a/c connections a day with **Bangkok**. The road south to **Mae Sot**, following the Burmese border, though slow (6 hrs), is mainly in good repair although there are 1 or 2 places where it has been allowed to deteriorate.

Songthaew
Songthaews to local destinations, congregate at the morning market on Sathit Phon Rd.
   Songthaews depart 4 times a day from the bus station for **Mae Sot** (6 hrs, ฿200).

❶ Directory

Pai p61, map p62
Medical services Pai Hospital, Chai Songkhram Rd (about 500 m from the town centre).

Mae Hong Son p63, map p64
Immigration Khunlum Praphat Rd (northern end of town, towards Pai).
Medical services Clinic, Khunlum Praphat Rd. **Hospital**, at the eastern end of Singhanat Bamrung Rd. **Police** Tourist Police: 1 Rachathampitak Rd, T053-611812 (claim 24 hrs service).

Chiang Rai and around

Given the ancient roots of Chiang Rai, the capital of Thailand's most northerly province, there's little here in the way of historical interest, with modern shophouse architecture predominating. What Chiang Rai lacks in sights it makes up for with a dose of rootsy, friendly charm and some great accommodation. It also makes a perfect base for trekking and to visit the towns further to the north.

West of the city are Ta Thon, a centre for rafting down to Chiang Rai and another good base for trekking. Fang, south of Ta Thon, has some good examples of shophouses, and is an opium trafficking centre.

Chiang Rai → *For listings, see pages 79-85.*

Chiang Rai was founded in 1268 by King Mengrai, who later moved his capital here. The city became one of the key *muang* (city states), within the Lanna Kingdom's sphere of control – until Lanna began to disintegrate in the 16th century. Although it is now Thailand's most northerly town, at the time of its foundation Chiang Rai represented the most southerly bulwark against the Mons. It was later conquered by the Burmese and only became part of Thailand again in 1786.

Today, Chiang Rai has ambitious plans for the future. Lying close to what has been termed the 'Golden Rectangle', linking Thailand with Laos, Burma (Myanmar) and southern China, the city's politicians and businessmen hope to cash in on the opening up of the latter three countries. Always searching for catchy phrases to talk up a nascent idea, they even talk of the 'Five Chiangs strategy' – referring to the five towns of Chiang Tung (or Kengtung in Burma), Chiang Rung (in China), Chiang Thong (in Laos), and Chiang Mai and Chiang Rai (both in Thailand). Roads linking the five are being planned and an EU-style free trade area discussed. Talk, as they say, is cheap; a mini-EU in this peripheral part of Asia seems a distant dream, despite a noticeable increase in cross-border activity.

Arriving in Chiang Rai

Getting there The international airport is 8 km north of the city, just off the main Chiang Rai–Mae Sai Highway. There's a pre-paid taxi stand in the airport from about ฿200 for a trip to the centre. A tuk-tuk to the airport from town is usually ฿150. The bus station is in the town centre just off Phahonyothin Road, T053-711224. The local *songthaew* stand is near the morning market on Uttarakit Road.

The new road to Chiang Rai from Chiang Mai cuts through forests and is fast and scenic. There are rather novel European-style country cottages along the way and some good resort-style hotels (see Where to stay, page 79). **Mae Suai**, with a hilltop monastery, is at the junction where roads lead south to Chiang Mai, north to Chiang Rai, west to Fang and southeast to Phayao. ▸▸ *See Transport, page 84, for further information.*

Getting around The centre of Chiang Rai is small enough to walk or cycle around but there are tuk tuks available from about ฿40. Most of the area's attractions lie in the surrounding countryside, and there are ample vehicle hire shops offering bicycles, cars, motorbikes and jeeps.

Tourist information TAT ⓘ *448/16 Singhaklai Rd (near the river, opposite Wat Phra Singh), T053-744674.* Well-run office with useful town maps and information on trekking and accommodation. Areas of responsibility are Chiang Rai, Phayao, Uttaradit, Phrae and Nan.

Places in Chiang Rai

The city's finest monastery is **Wat Phra Kaeo**, at the north end of Trairat Road. The wat is thought to have been founded in the 13th century when it was known as Wat Pa-Year. Its change of name came about following divine intervention in 1434 when, local legend recounts, the stupa was struck by lightning to reveal the famous Emerald Buddha or Phra Kaeo, now in residence in Bangkok's Temple of the Emerald Buddha. With this momentous discovery, the wat was renamed Wat Phra Kaeo and was elevated to the status of a royal wat in 1987.

The finest structure here is the *bot* (straight ahead as you pass through the main gates on Trairat Road) featuring accomplished woodcarving, a pair of fine *nagas* flanking the entrance way and, inside, a 13th-century image of the Buddha calling the earth goddess to witness. Presumably slightly peeved that the Phra Kaeo itself had been carted off to Bangkok, a rich local Chinese businessman – Mr Lo – commissioned a Chinese artist to carve a replica image from Canadian jade. The work was undertaken in Beijing to mark the 90th birthday of the Princess Mother and she gave it the gargantuan name Phraphuttaratanakorn Nawutiwatsanusornmongkhon, or The Lord Buddha is the source of the Three Gems of Buddhism. The image was kept in the monastery's *bot* until a new building, specially designed to house it, had been completed and the image installed in a consecration ceremony held in 1991. The Chiang Rai Phra Kaeo Shrine is behind the *bot*, with two ponds filled with turtles (set free by people to gain merit) in front of it.

Above Wat Phra Kaeo, perched at the top of a small hill, is **Wat Ngam Muang**, unremarkable except for the views it offers of the city and surrounding countryside. However, historically it is important, as the stupa here contains the ashes of the great King Mengrai (1259-1317). The edifice is currently being renovated and will have a statue of the king placed in front of his *ku*.

Further northwest still is **Wat Phrathat Doi Chom Thong**, built at the top of a small hill. The wat contains the *lak muang* (city pillar).

Wat Phra Singh (dating from 1385) is an important teaching monastery on Singhaklai Road, in the north of town. Note the finely wrought animal medallions below the windows of the *bot* – rats, elephants, tigers, snakes and other beasts – and the gaudy but vivacious murals that decorate the interior. Also unusual is the Bodhi tree, surrounded by images of the Buddha in each of the principal *mudras*.

South of Wat Phra Singh is **Wat Mung Muang**, notable for its corpulent image of the Buddha, which projects above the monastery walls. The image is not at all Thai in style, but appears Chinese with its sausage-like fingers spinning the wheel of law. The area around Wat Mung Muang supports a daily **market** and, in the mornings from 0600, vegetable hawkers set up along the monastery walls, providing a wonderful contrast in colour and texture with the golden Buddha image. *Songthaews, saamlors* and tuk-tuks wait to transport market-goers back to their houses and villages. In the east of town, at the so-called *haa yaek*

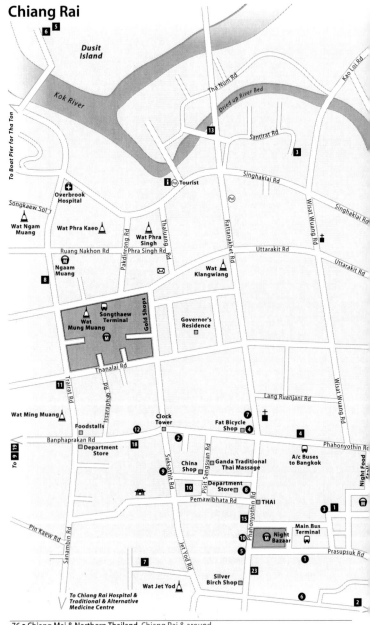

Chiang Rai

Dusit Island

Kok River

Tha Num Rd

Dried up River Bed

Santirat Rd

Kao Lol Rd

Singhaklai Rd

Singhaklai Rd

Wisat Wuang Rd

To Boat Pier for Tha Ton

Tourist

Overbrook Hospital

Songkaew Sol 1

Wat Ngam Muang

Wat Phra Kaeo

Ruang Nakhon Rd

Pakdinong Rd

Thaluang Rd

Wat Phra Singh

Phra Singh Rd

Uttarakit Rd

Uttarakit Rd

Ngaam Muang

Rattanakhet Rd

Wat Klangwiang

Wat Mung Muang

Songthaew Terminal

Gold Shops

Governor's Residence

Thanalai Rd

Traisit Rd

Issaraphab Rd

Wisat Wuang Rd

Lang Ruanjani Rd

Wat Ming Muang

Foodstalls

Banphaprakan Rd

Clock Tower

Fat Bicycle Shop

Department Store

To 9 19

China Shop

Suksathit Rd

Pisit Sangsuan Rd

Ganda Traditional Thai Massage

A/c Buses to Bangkok

Phahonyothin Rd

Night Food

Department Store

Pemawibhata Rd

THAI

Pin Kaew Rd

Sanambin Rd

Jet Yod Rd

Phahonyothin Rd

Night Bazaar

Main Bus Terminal

Prasupsuk Rd

Wat Jet Yod

Silver Birch Shop

To Chiang Rai Hospital & Traditional & Alternative Medicine Centre

Wat Sriboonruang

To Handcraft Centre,
Airport (8.5 km) & Mae Sai

To 12

Soi Koh Kaew

Sriboonruang Rd

Kong Yao Rd

King Mengrai's
Monument

Phahonyothin Rd

To Highway 1232

To Asy

Hill Tribe
Education Center

Nong Siijaeng Rd

To Wat Rong Khun
& Chiang Mai

N

100 metres
100 yards

Where to stay
Akha Guesthouse 13
B2 19
Baan Rub Aroon 8
Baan Wararbordee 2
Boonbundan
  Guesthouse 7
Chian House 14
Diamond Park Inn 17
Dusit Island 6
Golden Triangle Inn 4
La Vie En Rose 9
Le Méridien Chiang Rai 12

Legend Chiang Rai 5
Lek House 11
Mae Hong Son 3
North 1
Sukniran 18
Wangcome 10
Wiang Inn 23

Restaurants
Aye's Place 5
Baan Chivitmai 1
Doi Chaang 4
Kaffee Hub 2
La Vinci 10
Nakhom Pathom 8
Oasis 3
Por Jai 9
Ratburi 12
Vietnam 6
Work@home 7

(five-way junction) on Phahonyothin Road, is the new statue of King Mengrai, Chiang Rai's most illustrious king.

Building on the success of Chiang Mai's night bazaar or market, Chiang Rai opened its own **night bazaar** off Phahonyothin Road a few years back. It has since expanded tremendously and sells the usual range of hilltribe handicrafts, carvings, china products, wooden boxes, picture frames, the Thai equivalent of beanie babies, catapults and so on. In many ways it is a nicer place to browse than the Chiang Mai night bazaar. It is more open, less frenetic, friendlier, and there is live music and open-air restaurants.

About 10 km south towards Chiang Mai stands one of the north's newest and most popular temples, **Wat Rong Khun** ① *Mon-Fri 0800-1730, Sat and Sun 0800-1800, free.* Crafted by a local artist, this temple looks like it has been frosted white by a freezing Arctic storm – the entire construction is built in concrete, inlaid with mirrors and then whitewashed. Some might think the result is daring beauty – others could come to the conclusion it is kitsch trash dressed up as art. The general populous seems to love the place and at weekends queues of camera-phone-wielding Thais eagerly take snaps of their loved ones in front of this startling structure. If you want to judge for yourself take a *songthaew* (every 30 minutes) from the centre of Chiang Rai to Mae Lao and get off at the temple (฿30). Alternatively hire a tuk-tuk for a half-day excursion (฿300-400).

The **Hilltribe Education Center** ① *620/ 25 Thanalai Rd, 1300-1330, or on request, for a small fee, in English, Thai, French or Japanese,* is one of the more interesting attractions in the town, with a small, informative **hilltribe museum** ① *0830-2000; admission to museum ฿20, CRPDA@hotmail.com,* and an audiovisual presentation on hilltribe life. It is run by the Population and Development Association's (PDA), which is better known for its family planning and AIDS work. With this project, it is attempting to provide hilltribe communities with additional income-earning opportunities, as the pressures of commercial life increase. The museum has recently been expanded and refurbished. Attached to the museum is a branch of the **Cabbages and Condoms** chain of restaurants.

Ban Du is a paper-making village, 8 km north of Chiang Rai off Route 110. Paper is produced from the bark of the sa tree, which is stripped off, air dried, soaked in water, boiled in caustic soda and finally beaten, before being made into paper.

West of Chiang Rai → *For listings, see pages 79-85.*

From Chiang Rai a road winds westwards over the mountains towards Tha Ton where boats and rafts can be hired to travel down the Kok River to Chiang Rai. Beyond Tha Ton on Route 107 is the former strategic town of Fang.

Tha Ton
Tha Ton lies on the Mae Kok and is a good starting point for trips on the Kok River to Chiang Rai, and for treks to the various hilltribe villages in the area. It is a pleasant little town with good accommodation and a friendly atmosphere. It also makes a good base for exploring this area of the north. Rafts travel downstream to Chiang Rai, while by road it is possible to head towards Doi Mae Salong, Mae Sai and Chiang Saen. Remember to alight at the junction of Routes 1095 and 107 and then catch one of the regular buses heading north to Fang.

Wat Tha Ton overlooks the river, not far from the bridge. A stairway leads up to this schizophrenic monastery. On the hillside is a rather ersatz Chinese grotto, with gods, goddesses and fantastic animals including Kuan Yin, the monkey god and entwined dragons. From this little piece of China, the stairway emerges in the compound of a classic, but rather ugly, modern Theravada Buddhist monastery. There is a restaurant, souvenir stall and more to show that Wat Tha Ton has truly embraced the pilgrim's dollar (or baht).

The boat trip to and from Chiang Rai takes three to four hours (฿350) on the daily scheduled public boat. You can also rent a private long-tail for up to six people to Chiang Rai (A2200). ▸▸ *See What to do, page 83, and Transport, page 85.*

The regular boat down the Kok River stops at riverside villages, from where it is possible to trek to hilltribe communities. **Louta**, 14 km east of Tha Ton and 1.5 km off the main road between Tha Ton and Doi Mae Salong/Chiang Rai, is a well-off, developed Lisu village. It's also possible to get here by yellow pick-up (14 km), then take a motorbike taxi the remaining 1500 m uphill.

Other nearby villages include: **Tahamakeng**, one hour from Tha Ton (Lahu and Lisu villages within easy reach); **Ban Mai**, 45 minutes on from Tahamakeng (Lahu, Karen and Akha villages); and Mae Salak, further on still (Lahu, Lisu and Yao villages). ▸▸ *See What to do, page 83.*

Fang
Fang was once a lawless centre for the trafficking of opium; now it is known for its orange groves and nearby tea terraces. Though it is not a major tourist destination, it retains a distinctive frontier feel, cut off by a ring of distant rising hills, the rows of whisky bars and karaoke clubs attesting to its unruly element.

It was founded by King Mengrai in the 13th century, although its strategic location at the head of a valley means it has probably been an important trading settlement for centuries.

The government has had some success in encouraging the predominantly Yao hilltribes to switch from opium production to other cash crops such as cabbages and potatoes. Some of the old drug business persists but compared to years gone by it is relatively marginal. The valley surrounding Fang is particularly fertile and is used for rice, fruit and vegetable cultivation. The Fang Oil Refinery, on Route 109, also provides employment.

There is a good smattering of traditional wooden shophouses in town. The bus station is on the main road in the centre of town. Wat Jong Paen, on Tha Phae Road at the northern edge of town, is Burmese in style. The best day to be in Fang is Wednesday – market day – when colourful hill peoples come to town to sell crops, textiles and more. The market winds down from 1300.

The *bor nam rawn* or **hot springs** can be found 12 km west of Fang, near Ban Muang Chom. To get there, turn left shortly after leaving the town on the road north to Tha Ton.

Chiang Rai and around listings

For hotel and restaurant price codes and other relevant information, see pages 8-12.

🛏 Where to stay

Chiang Rai *p74, map p76*
Accommodation in Chiang Rai is of a high standard. Guesthouses, in particular, are quiet, with large and generally clean rooms – a welcome change from some places in Chiang Mai. Most are concentrated in the quieter northern part of the city, some on the 'island' between both branches of the Kok River.

$$$$ Dusit Island, 1129 Kraisorasit Rd, T053-607999, chiangrai.dusit.com. Overblown, fairly ostentatious hotel, just north of town on an 'island' in the river, set in lavish grounds. 271 a/c rooms and suites, and every facility including restaurant, fitness centre, tennis courts, pool and spa.

$$$$ The Legend Chiang Rai, 124/15 Kohloy Rd, T053-910400, www.thelegend-chiangrai.com. A spacious contemporary Lanna-style boutique hotel on the banks of the Mae Kok River, just a few mins' drive north from the centre of town

$$$$ Le Méridien Chiang Rai, 221/2 Moo 20 Kwaewai Rd, T053-603-333, www.le meridienchiangrai.com. Built around 2 giant old raintrees, this expansive modern Lanna-style 5-star sits on the Mae Kok River's banks. Despite an off-the-peg brand hotel feel, it's chic and impressive, especially the raised lobby/terrace overlooking the resort's infinity swimming pool, big lake and lush riverside backdrop. Every room has a private balcony. Free shuttle service into town. Excellent dining, gym and spa. Recommended.

$$$$-$$$ Wangcome Hotel, 869/90 Pemawibhata Rd, T053-711800, www. wangcome.com. Reasonable hotel in a great central location. Each room is a/c and en suite with minibar and TV. Restaurant, bar and karaoke on site. Huge suites if you can afford them.

$$$-$$ Diamond Park Inn, 74/6 Moo 18, Sanpanard Rd, T053-754960, www.diamond parkinn.com. Good-value hotel down the end of a quiet *soi* a short walk from the night bazaar. All rooms are en suite with a/c. The larger 'de luxe' rooms are the best value. Also has a restaurant.

$$$-$$ Golden Triangle Inn, 590 Phahonyothin Rd, T053-711339. A/c, restaurant. This is a great little hotel on a tree-filled plot of land, rooms are clean and stylish with hot water. Good treks, friendly atmosphere, breakfast included in room rate. Recommended.

$$$-$$ La Vie En Rose, 92/9 Ratchayotha Rd, T053-601351, www.lavieenrosehotel. com. Imposing white structure, set back in manicured gardens from the main road. Friendly, decent service, with large, nicely decorated modern rooms with all the extras you'd expect in this price range: a/c, bathtubs, Wi-Fi breakfast and flat-screen TVs.

\$\$\$-\$\$ Wiang Inn, 893 Phahonyothin Rd, T053-711533. The original 'luxury' hotel in town, renovated in 1992-1993 and still holding its own. Competitively priced, central location but set back from the main road so comparatively peaceful, stylish lobby. Rooms are fairly standard, but perfectly adequate with satellite TV. A/c, restaurant, small pool, The buffet breakfast and lunch (with dim sum) are very good value. Recommended.

\$\$-\$ Akha River House, 423/25 Moo 21 Kohloy Rd (behind the TAT office), T053-715084, www.chiangrairiverhouse.com. Run by Akha tribespeople, this peaceful guesthouse sits beside a bridge and a thin, dry tributary of the Mae Kok River. A few mins' drive north of the night market. Pick from the basic, budget fan rooms in a rustic Thai house or stylish a/c rooms in a newer 2-storey mud-wash building, with adobe-style walls, big bathrooms, riverside terraces and TVs. Helpful staff.

\$\$-\$ B2 Hotel, 362/3 Charoenrajd Rd, T053-242838, www.b2hotel.com. This is an attempt to create a budget designer hotel. The rooms are decent enough, with some artistic flourishes, dark woods and the like, all a/c, en suite, with flat-screen TVs and Wi-Fi. The problem is the service, which is very poor. For the price though, it's still a pretty good deal.

\$\$-\$ Baan Rub Aroon Guesthouse, 65 Ngam-muang Rd, T053-711827, www.baanrubaroon.net. An old whitewashed town villa, set in its own private grounds, this charming guesthouse has a variety of airy, well-lit rooms and a friendly, homestay ambience. There's a kitchen for guests' use and Wi-Fi. Bathroom facilities are shared. Lots of communal hang-out spaces. Recommended.

\$\$-\$ Baan Wararbordee, 59/1 Moo 18, Sanpanard Rd, T053-754888. Delightful little guesthouse tucked away on a quiet soi. Very friendly, helpful owner, free coffee,

tea and internet. Rooms on the upper floors are better lit – all have TV, en suite, hot water and a/c. There's a garden as well. Recommended.

\$\$-\$ Boonbundan Guesthouse, 1005/13 Jet Yod Rd, T053-717040. Quiet leafy compound near the centre of town. Professionally managed, good range of services, clean rooms with hot water although becoming shabby. Some a/c, outdoor eating area. Recommended, including the tours.

\$\$-\$ Chian House, 172 Sriboonruang Rd, on the island, T053-713388. Clean and friendly – the large bungalows are especially good value. Peaceful atmosphere and good food. Also organizes treks and tours and has internet.

\$\$-\$ Lek House, 95 Thanalai Rd, T053-713337. Well-organized, friendly place, with a bar and food and satellite TV. Rents out motorbikes.

\$\$-\$ Mae Hong Son, 126 Singhaklai Rd, T053-715367. Friendly Dutch-run guesthouse at the end of a very quiet soi. The traditional wooden house has clean rooms with shared bathrooms; newer rooms have en suite but are more expensive. Treks (recommended, with a great guide), jeep and motorbike hire, good source of information. Peaceful and good value. Tasty food. Recommended.

\$\$-\$ The North Hotel, small soi just behind the bus station, T053-719873, www.thenorth.co.th. A funky little hotel with library, roof terrace, bar and restaurant. It has seen better days but is still a good location. Rooms are a/c and en suite.

\$\$-\$ Sukniran, 424/1 Banphaprakan Rd, T053-711955. Some a/c, good position close to clock tower, airy lobby and rooms facing a courtyard away from the main road, so not too noisy. Go for rooms at the back.

Tha Ton p78

For some reason Tha Ton's popularity has waned of late and several of the long-standing accommodation options have closed down. There are still some great places to stay here though.

$$$$-$$$ Maekok Village Resort, on road to Mae Salong, 1.5 km before the bridge, T053-053628, www.maekok-river-village-resort.com. Well-run and well-appointed riverside resort with beautiful gardens, decent-sized swimming pool and a quiet location. Rooms are huge, upmarket and stylish, with en suite, a/c and TVs. Restaurant is decidedly average but this is the most luxurious resort by far in town.

$$$-$$ Khunmai Baansuan Resort, 13 Moo 14, T053-373214, www.khunmai baansuan.com. Located beside the river in a dramatic setting beneath towering cliffs about 1 km out of town, this family-run establishment has a suitably relaxing vibe. Rooms are either slightly overpriced riverside bungalows or set in a small block behind the restaurant. All are en suite and a/c with TVs.

$$$-$$ Old Trees House, on road to Mae Salong, 1 km before bridge, T08-5722 9002, www.oldtreeshouse.net. Eccentric collection of 4 cute bungalows in this entrancing hill-top resort. There's a small pool, stunning views and great food and wine. Rooms are fairly basic but comfortable, and there are plenty of day beds and the like for people to recline on, scattered around this friendly set-up. Recommended.

$$$-$ Garden Home, T053-373015. Away from the main bustle, this peaceful resort has bungalows set in a large tree-filled orchard garden on the river's edge. Spotlessly clean rooms range widely in price from guesthouse level up to hotel quality. Quiet and friendly, no restaurant. Recommended.

$ Naam Waan Guesthouse, Soi Udomphon, T053-459403. Small, clean, simple rooms set around a courtyard. Friendly.

Fang p78

$$$$-$$ Angkhang Nature Resort, 40 km west of Fang, on Route 1249, 1/1 Moo 5 Baan Koom, Tambon Mae Ngon, T053-450110, www.amari.com/angkhang. Situated high in the cool mountains very close to the border with Burma, the resort was developed under the auspices of the

Royal Project Foundation. It consists of 72 well-appointed rooms with all mod-cons.

$$$-$$ Tangerine Ville Hotel, 117 Moo 2 Sansai, T053-882600. Decent enough hotel a couple of kilometres south of town on the road to Chiang Mai. Rooms offer the standard TV, hot water and a/c facilities you'd expect while not much character. Rate also includes breakfast.

$$-$ Baan Fanh Hotel, 49 Moo 3 Tapae Rd, T053-451281. Small hotel set back from the main road. Friendly with a stylish feel. All rooms are a/c with en suite and hot water. Free Wi-Fi and a basic, self-service breakfast. Good value.

$$-$ Baan Sa-Bai Hotel, 88 Moo 9, Wieng Fang. Set almost behind the new Tesco Lotus in a very quiet soi, this is very relaxed place to stay. Rooms are simple, spotless and well kept, all with TV, hot showers, a/c etc. Good choice if you need a rest.

$$-$ Phumanee Home Hotel, 122/ 1 Moo 4, T053-452875. Friendly, though now slightly run-down, family-run hotel in centre of Fang. Rooms are en suite and come with a/c or fan, and there is free Wi-Fi available. Breakfast is included. Go for rooms on top floors as there are good views of the local hills. Also sell decent Thai food in a small restaurant.

Restaurants

Chiang Rai *p74, map p76*
The greatest variety of restaurants is to be found in the streets around the **Wangcome Hotel**, from Mexican to French to cheap Thai and Chinese. Many of the tourist-oriented restaurants serve the same range of dishes: wiener schnitzel, lasagne, pizza, burgers, fried rice. At night, head to the food stalls in the night bazaar, although the quality here isn't exceptional. Locals also frequent the stalls past the clock tower on Bangpharakan Rd.

$$$ La Vinci, 879/4-6 Phahonyothin Rd, opposite entrance to the night bazaar. Decent enough, if overpriced, wood-fired pizzas and passable attempts at Italian food provide something for those bored of spicy food.

$$ Chiangrai Island Restaurant, 1129/1 Kraisorasit Rd (part of **Dusit Island Hotel**). Northern Thai specialities, also serves international food.

$$ Ratanakosin, T053-740012. Open 1600-2400. Highly recommended for quality of food and atmospheric decor. Faces onto the night bazaar, so you can feel part of the action, and dine from the upstairs balcony, whilst watching the Thai dancing below.

$$ Vietnam Restaurant, Sanpanard Rd. Easy to spot, funky wooden building down this quiet soi. Run by an artist, with slightly random opening hours. The food is excellent and authentic. Recommended.

$$-$ Baan Chivitmai, just opposite the bus station. Run by a Swedish Christian charity, this is a perfect spot to gather your thoughts, chomp on a yummy cake and sup on a decent coffee before setting off around town. Great breakfasts and good juices keep this place full, but it's a little pricey.

$$-$ Doi Chaang, Banphapraken Rd. An outlet for a community-controlled coffee-growing project that is well worth supporting, if only for the fact that they serve a great cup of the brown, roasted stuff. Decent cakes as well.

$$-$ Kaffee Hub, opposite the clock tower on Bangphaprakan Rd, T08-2574 5999. Daily 0800-0100. Decent coffee, some ok Thai food and average cake but a neat hang-out location. Stays open late when it transforms into a bar.

$$-$ Work@Home, 545 Rattanakhet Rd, T053-714619. Mon-Sat 0800-2000, Sun 1200-2000. Coffee, cakes, snacks, hot chocolate. Open layout and road-side seats complete with Wi-Fi make this a great little place to relax.

$ Aye's Place, Phahonyothin Rd, opposite entrance to **Wiang Inn**, T053-752535. Spacious restaurant open for breakfast (though not very early), lunch and dinner, extensive Thai and international menu. The baguettes are particularly good.

$ Nakhon Pathom (Thai signage only), 869/25 Phahonyothin Rd, T053-713617. Daily 0600-1500. Excellent and popular shophouse-style restaurant selling great noodles, BBQ pork and crispy pork-belly over rice. Gets packed with locals at breakfast time. Recommended.

$ Oasis, back soi behind bus station, 0800-1800. Scrummy vegetarian food, including plenty of tofu dishes served here.

$ Por Jai, Jed Yod Rd (behind **Wiang Come Hotel**). Daily 0600-1700. One of the best khao soy shops in Chiang Rai, popular with locals and highly recommended.

$ Ratburi, Banphaprakan Rd, opposite **Sukniran Hotel**. Large selection of curries, eat in or takeaway, ฿15 per dish.

Tha Ton *p78*

There are a few small cafés selling backpacker fare by the river and on the main road. You can also find a couple of excellent Thai food places on the road by the pier.

$ Khao Soi Restaurant, right by the river and bridge, and next to **Thip's Travellers House**. Friendly place serving *khao soi* (of course) and the usual rice and noodle dishes.

Fang *p78*

$ JJ's Bakery, opposite Wat Chedi Ngam on the main road. Cakes, Thai and international.

$ Muang Fang, on the main road, next to the Bangkok Bank. Typical Thai food.

🎵 Bars and clubs

Chiang Rai *p74, map p76*
There's now a burgeoning bar scene in Chiang Rai – many can be found down Jet Yod Rd.

Easy House Bar and Restaurant, Permaviphat Rd (opposite **Wangcome Hotel**). Cocktails, beers, live music, self-consciously hip.

Lobo Bar, down a narrow private *soi* off Phahonyothin Rd, near the clock tower. A lively place.

Teepee Bar, Phahonyothin Rd. Interesting-looking backpacker hang-out. Look for the old beaten-up motorbike.

⊙ Shopping

Chiang Rai *p74, map p76*
Books
Pho Thong Book Store, Thanalai Rd (close to the intersection with Trairat Rd). Mostly in Thai, but some English books and magazines.

China
China shop, Pisit Sangsuan Rd. Thai-decorated seconds for US and UK shops (such as **Whittards**), on sale here at rock-bottom prices. Mugs, bowls, plates and teapots.

Department stores
Edision department store, on the corner of Banphraprakan and Sanambin roads. Also an a/c department store near the **Wangcome Hotel**, on the corner of Phahonyothin and Pemavipat roads.

Handicrafts, silver and textiles
Many shops in town around the **Wangcome Hotel** plaza area and on Phahonyothin Rd sell hilltribe goods, silver, textiles and woodcarvings. See also Night market, below.
Chiang Rai Handicrafts Centre, 3 km out of town on road to Chiang Saen.
Hilltribe Education Center, 620/25 Thanalai Rd. Sells genuine hilltribe textiles and other goods, all profits go back to the communities.
Silver Birch, 891 Phahonyothin Rd, near **Wiang Inn**. For unusual woodcarvings and silverware, more expensive but finely crafted.

Music
There is a great little music shop near the clock tower at the northern end of Jet Yod Rd.

Night market
There is a night bazaar just off Phahonyothin Rd, close to the bus terminal. The stalls and shops sell a range of goods, including hilltribe handicrafts, silverware, woodcarvings, T-shirts, clothes, pin cushions, Burmese bags and leatherware. Foodstalls and bars open in the evening.

⊙ What to do

Chiang Rai *p74, map p76*
Sports clubs
Pintamorn Sportsclub, 115/1-8 Wat Sriboonruang Rd. Sauna, exercise room, pool table.

Therapies
There are several places in the network of streets near the **Wangcome Hotel**, and **Wat Jet Yod** offers traditional Thai massage from ฿200 per hr.
Traditional & Alternative Medicine Centre, opposite Chiang Rai Regional Hospital, Satharn Payabarn Rd. Mon-Fri 0800-1600. One of the best massages in town is available in this centre run as part of the local hospital. Foot massage is ฿150 per hr, while 90 mins of Thai massage is ฿200. Recommended.

Tours and trekking
Most treks are cheaper if organized through guesthouses, and they are usually also more adventurous. The usual range of **elephant rides** and **boat trips** as part of a trek are available, too. A 2-day/1-night **raft trip** costs ฿800-1100 per person, 4-day/3-night **trek** about ฿1500-2000. Day tours to visit **hilltribe villages** such as Sop Ruak and the Golden Triangle, Mae Sai, Mae Salong and Chiang Saen, are organized by most of the tour/trekking companies listed below (฿600). Tours that include an elephant ride and boat trip, plus visits to hilltribe villages, cost about ฿700. **Motorcycle tours** are also becoming increasingly popular, and many guesthouses provide rental services and information on routes to take for a day's excursion. Before embarking on a trek, it is worth visiting the **Hilltribe Education Center** (see page 77). Tribes in the area include Karen, Lisu, Lahu and Akha.

There are several trekking companies and tour operators around the **Wangcome Hotel** plaza area, along Phahonyothin and Premwipak roads (a *soi* off Phahonyothin). The **TAT** office produces a list of companies with average prices and other useful advice. **Golden Triangle Tours**, 590 Phahonyothin Rd, T053-711339 (attached to the **Golden Triangle Hotel**). Recommended. **Mae Salong Tour**, 882/4 Phahonyothin Rd, T053-712515. Recommended treks, also organizes river cruises on the Mekong including Laos, China and Thailand. **PDA**, 620/25 Thanalai Rd, T053-719167. Primarily a charity, working to improve the lot of the hilltribes but also runs treks – all profits are ploughed back into the charity. Treks introduce clients to the PDA's community development projects; guides tend to be very knowledgeable about hilltribe customs. Advance booking recommended.

Also try **Chiangrai Agency Centre**, 428/10 Banpha-prakan Rd, T053-717274, or **Chiangrai Travel and Tour**, 869/95 Premwipak Rd, T053-713314.

Cycling

Fat Bike Shop, 542/2 Banphaprakan Rd, T053-752532. Well-maintained mountain and road bikes for rental. Prices start at ฿100 for 24 hrs.

⊖ Transport

Chiang Rai *p74, map p76*
Air
THAI, Nokand Air Asia provide Regular connections with **Chiang Mai** (40 mins) and **Bangkok** (1 hr 25 mins). The runway has been lengthened to take wide-bodied jets, and there is some talk of the possibility of international connections in the near future with other Asian destinations.

Airline offices THAI, 870 Phahonyothin Rd, T053-711179.

Bicycle
Guesthouses offer hire for ฿20-40 per day.

Boat
Long-tailed boats leave from the new pier, 2 km northwest of the centre; follow Trairat Rd north, past the entrance to the **Dusit Island Resort**, to the T-junction with Winitchakun Rd. Turn right and continue past the golf course to the bridge over the Kok River. The pier is on the far side of the river. Boats for **Tha Ton** depart daily at 1000 (฿350). Boats can be chartered for ฿2200 to Tha Ton. A boat takes a maximum of 6 passengers, the pier is open daily 0700-1600.

Bus
Regular connections with **Chiang Saen** every 15 mins (1½ hrs) and **Mae Sai** every 15 mins (1 hr 40 mins), **Chiang Mai** (3 hrs), **Phayao** (1 hr 40 mins), **Phrae** (4 hrs), **Nan** (6 hrs), **Chiang Kham** (2 hrs), **Chiang Khong** (3 hrs), **Lampang** (5 hrs), **Phitsanulok** via Sukhothai (6 hrs), **Khon Kaen** (12 hrs), **Nakhon Ratchasima** (13 hrs), **Bangkok** (12 hrs), **Fang, Mae Suai, Nakhon Sawan, Sukhothai, Nakhon Phanom, Udon Thani** and **Pattaya**.

To **Chiang Mai**, buses taking the *sai kao* (old route) go via Phayao (6 hrs) and Lampang; buses taking the new road along Route 1019, go via Wiang Papao hot springs (4 hrs) and Doi Saket.

Car
Hire can be arranged through one of the many tour and travel companies around the **Wangcome Hotel**, or from **Budget**, based at the **Golden Triangle Inn**.

Jeep hire is ฿800 per day from many guesthouses, eg Bowling Guesthouse, Chian House, Pintamorn, Mae Hong Son Guesthouse and many tour companies.

Motorbike
Motorbike hire costs ฿150-200 per day, from most guesthouses and tour companies. **ST Motorcycle**, 1025/34-35 Jet Yod, T053-713652. One of the best motorcycle rental services in Northern Thailand, and one of the only places that will allow you (after a

large deposit has been taken) to cross into Laos and Burma. The owner, Khun Seksit, is friendly and straight talking. In addition to the ubiquitous step-throughs, he also has a fleet of well-maintained 250-600cc off-road bikes for the more serious motorcyclist. Highly recommended if biking is your thing.

Tha Ton p78
Boat
The boat to **Chiang Rai** departs at 1230 and takes 3-4½ hrs, depending on the state of the river (฿350). **Tha Ton Boat Office**, by the river, T053-459427, is open 0900-1500.

It's possible to hire an entire boat (seating up to 6 people) to **Chiang Rai** for ฿2200.

Bus
Regular connections with **Bangkok**, most leaving in the evening. Buses run to **Chiang Mai** (4 hrs), or take a minibus to **Fang** (45 mins), which has more frequent connections with Chiang Mai (3 hrs). To get to **Pai/Mae Hong Son** without going through Chiang Mai, catch a bus through Fang heading for Chiang Mai and get off at Ban Mae Malai, at the junction with Rte 1095. Then, pick up a bus heading for Pai/Mae Hong Son.

Songthaew
Connections with **Fang** every 15 mins. *Songthaews* also run to **Mae Salong** 4 to 6 times a day (90 mins) and to **Mae Chan** (2 hrs) from where you can connect with buses to **Chiang Rai** and **Mae Sai**.

Fang p78
Bus
Regular connections with **Chiang Mai** from the Chang Puak bus station on Chotana Rd, 3 hrs. Minibuses run on the hour through the week from next to the hospital to Chiang Mai (฿80).

Songthaew
Regular connections with **Tha Ton** (40 mins). There are 2 routes to Chiang Rai: either take the *songthaew* from Fang to Mae Suai (40 mins), then catch a bus to **Chiang Rai** (95 km), or take a *songthaew* from Tha Ton to Mae Chan, then on to Chiang Rai (114 km).

Chiang Saen and the Golden Triangle

Chiang Saen, northeast of Chiang Rai on the banks of the mighty Mekong River, was once the evocative capital of an ancient kingdom. Follow the meandering Mekong downstream and the road reaches the small outpost of Chiang Khong, home of the giant catfish and a crossing point into Laos. Meanwhile, 11 km upstream from Chiang Saen, is the infamous Golden Triangle, the meeting point of Laos, Thailand and Burma. This was once a lawless area filled with smugglers and drug lords. These days it's home to the tourist village of Sop Ruak and the compelling Opium Museum. Still further upstream, 61 km north of Chiang Rai, Mae Sai is Thailand's most northerly town and a busy border trading post with Burma. From Route 110 you can turn off and reach the hill town of Mae Salong, from where you can continue west to Tha Ton.

Chiang Saen → *For listings, see pages 92-97.*

Chiang Saen is an ancient capital on the banks of the Mekong River, the last village before the famed 'Golden Triangle'. Today, with the impressive town ramparts still very much in evidence, it is a charming one-street market town. The city walls run along three sides of the town and are pierced by five gates. The fourth 'wall' is formed by the Mekong River. Quiet, with wooden shophouses and a scattering of ruins lying haphazardly and untended in the undergrowth, it has so far managed to escape the uncontrolled tourist development of other towns in northern Thailand, but is now establishing itself as a river port, with large boats and barges bringing goods from China.

Arriving in Chiang Saen

Getting there and around Buses arrive regularly from Chiang Rai (one hour 20 minutes), Mae Sai and Chiang Khong. Long-tailed boats ply the Mekong River connecting Chiang Saen with Sop Ruak, Chiang Khong and Jin Hang in China. Motorized *saamlors* congregate by the bus stop and offer trips around the sights. ▶▶ *See Transport, page 97, for further information.*

Tourist information TAT ⓘ *Phahonyothin Rd, opposite the National Museum, 0830-1630,* is attached to the sensitively designed Bureau for the Restoration and Conservation of the Historic City of Chiang Mai.

Background

Chiang Saen was probably established during the early years of the last millennium and became the capital of the Chiang Saen Kingdom, founded in 1328 by King Saen Phu, the grandson of King Mengrai. Captured in the 16th century by the Burmese, the town became a Burmese stronghold in their constant wars with the Thais. It was not recaptured until Rama I sent an army here in 1803. Fearing that the Burmese might use the town to mount raids against his kingdom in the future, Rama I ordered it to be destroyed. Chiang Saen remained deserted for nearly 100 years. King Mongkut ordered the town to be repopulated, but it still feels as though it is only part-filled, its inhabitants rattling around in the area's illustrious history. The ancient city is a gazetted historic monument managed by the Thai Fine Arts Department, and in total there are 75 monasteries and other monuments inside the city walls and another 66 outside.

In September 1992, a 120-tonne ship, with 60 Chinese delegates aboard, made the 385-km trip down the Mekong from Yunnan. Since then, links with China – as well as Laos – have developed apace. Cargo boats unload apples and other produce from China, and the market in Chiang Saen is stocked with low-quality manufactured goods. Anticipating a trade boom, two new piers were built (one of which was promptly washed away) as well as a luxurious business centre south of town – demonstrating how much money there is around as people try to cash in on the 'Golden Quadrangle' (Thailand, Burma, Laos and China). These days a mini-river port is now developing in Chiang Saen and it is becoming an important hub for the import of Chinese goods. The road to Mae Sai and the Burmese border is being redeveloped into a four-lane highway, and this sleepy corner of Thailand will soon be transformed.

Places in Chiang Sean

Entering the town from Chiang Rai, the ruins of **Wat Phrathat Chedi Luang** can be seen on the right-hand side shortly after passing through the city's ancient ramparts. Built by King Saen Phu in 1331, this wat was established as the main monastery in the city. The *chedi*, resting on an octagonal base, is 60 m tall, but has fallen into disrepair over the centuries and is now clothed in long grass. The *viharn* is in a similar state of decrepitude and is protected by a jury-rigged corrugated-iron roof.

Just to the west of Wat Phrathat Chedi Luang is a small branch of the **National Museum** ① *Wed-Sun 0900-1200, 1300-1600, ฿10*. It contains various Buddha images and other artefacts unearthed in the area, as well as a small display of hilltribe handicrafts including clothing and musical instruments. Of the Buddha images, the most significant are those in the so-called Chiang Saen style, with their oval faces and slender bodies. They are regarded by art historians as being among the first true 'Thai' works of art.

West of town, just outside the city ramparts, is the beautiful **Wat Pa Sak** ① *฿30*, or 'Forest of Teak Wat' – so-called because of a wall of 300 teak trees, planted around the wat when it was founded. The monastery was founded in 1295 during the reign of Ramkhamhaeng of Sukhothai and actually predates the town. The unusual pyramid-shaped *chedi*, said to house a bone relic of the Lord Buddha, is the main building of interest here. Art historians see a combination of influences in the *chedi*: Pagan (Burma), Dvaravati, Sukhothai, and even Srivijaya. The niches along the base contain alternating *devatas* (heavenly beings) and standing Buddha images – poorly restored – the latter in the mudra of the Buddha 'Calling for Rain' (an attitude common in Laos but less so in Thailand). Much of the fine stucco work, save for fragments of *nagas* and *garudas*, has disappeared (some can be seen in the Chiang Saen Museum). The Spirit House at the entrance, by the ramparts, is also worth a little more than a glance.

On a hill 2.5 km north of Wat Pa Sak, following the ramparts, is **Wat Phrathat Chom Kitti**, which may date from as early as the 10th century. A golden-topped stupa is being

Opium of the people

The Golden Triangle is synonymous with the cultivation of the opium poppy. It is a favourite cash crop of the Lahu, Lisu, Mien and Hmong (the Karen and Akha only rarely grow it) and the attractions are clear: it is profitable, can be grown at high altitudes (above 1500 m), has low bulk (important when there is no transport) and does not rot. This explains why, though cultivation has been banned in Thailand since 1959, it has only been since the 1980s that the Thai government, with US assistance, has significantly reduced the poppy crop. Today, most opium is grown in Burma and Laos. In 2001 the UN estimated opium production in the Golden Triangle amounted to a total of 1260 tonnes of which 1087 tonnes was produced in Burma, 167 tonnes in Laos and just six tonnes in Thailand. This latter figure is not even sufficient for opium consumption by the hill peoples themselves.

The opium poppy is sown in September/October (the end of the wet season) and 'harvesting' stretches from the beginning of January through to the end of March. The petals then drop off and the remaining 'pod' is then carefully scoured with a sharp knife. The sap oozes out, oxidizes into a brown gum – raw opium – which is scraped off, rolled into balls and wrapped in banana leaves. It is now ready for sale.

Though profitable, opium has not benefited the hilltribes. In the government's eyes they are criminals, and opium addiction is widespread – up to 30% in some areas. Efforts to change the ways of the hilltribes have focused upon crop substitution programmes and simple intimidation.

restored, but there is little else save for the views of the river and surrounding countryside. **Wat Chom Cheung**, a small ruined *chedi*, lies close by on the same hill. If visiting by foot, the stairs start about 150 m from the city walls and come first to Wat Chom Cheung. A highly decorated new wat has recently been completed here.

Strung out along the riverbank, the market sells plenty of unnecessary plastic objects and is a good place to watch hilltribe people (Karen and Lua among others) browsing through the goods. Since trade with China and Laos has expanded, it is also possible to pick up cheap – but poorly made – products from 'across the water'.

Wat Phrathat Pa Ngao, lies 4 km from Chiang Saen, along the road that follows the Mekong downstream. Perched on a hill, it provides views of the river and countryside. For Sop Ruak and the Golden Triangle take the same road upstream, 11 km from town (see below). Take a *songthaew* or long-tailed boat; boats can be hired from the jetty below the **Salathai Restaurant** and will also take passengers to riverside villages (bargain hard).

Sop Ruak → *For listings, see pages 92-97.*

This small 'village', 11 km north of Chiang Saen at the apex of the Golden Triangle, where Burma, Laos and Thailand meet, has become a busy tourist spot on the basis (largely unwarranted) of its association with drugs, intrigue and violence. It's actually rather dull, with rows of tacky stalls selling hilltribe handicrafts and Burmese and Laotian goods, and a succession of maps and marble constructions informing visitors they are at the Golden Triangle. Two first-class hotels have been built to exploit the supposed romance of the place.

For those searching for something else to experience, **Wat Prathat Phukaeo** provides good views of the Golden Triangle. The **Hall of Opium** ① *just outside town opposite the gate to the Anantara, Tue-Sun 0830-1600, ฿300,* charts the rise of the international opium trade – largely put in place by 19th-century British businessmen with the backing of the British government – and the contemporary effects of the narcotics trade.

Wanglao, 4 km west towards Mae Sai, is a rice-farming community. It is sometimes possible to buy handicrafts here. *Songthaews* run through here on the (longer) back route to Mae Sai.

Boats can be chartered from the riverbank for trips downstream to Chiang Saen (฿400 for five people, 30 minutes), or further on still to Chiang Khong (around ฿1500-1700, 1½ hours). Alternatively they can be chartered just to explore the Golden Triangle area.

Chiang Khong → *For listings, see pages 92-97.*

This border settlement, on the south bank of the Mekong, is really more a collection of villages than a town: Ban Haad Khrai, Ban Sobsom and Ban Hua Wiang were all originally individual communities – and still retain their village monasteries. For such a small town, it has had a relatively high profile in Thai history. In the 1260s, King Mengrai extended control over the area and Chiang Khong became one of the Lanna Thai Kingdom's major principalities. Later, the town was captured by the Burmese.

The area's popularity is due to its proximity to a border crossing into Laos – just the other side of the river. These days large ferries carrying giant trucks cross here and, as of mid-2013, a new bridge is near completion, something that will make the ferry service redundant. Boats from the Laos town of Huay Xai, on the opposite side, travel downriver to the ancient city of Luang Prabang. Aside from that, Chiang Khong has a relaxed atmosphere making it an attractive spot to unwind.

Getting around

Chiang Khong is small enough to explore on foot. Bicycles and motorbikes are available for hire from guesthouses.

Places in Chiang Khong

Wat Luang, in the centre of town, dates from the 13th century. An engraved plaque maintains that two hairs of the Buddha were interred in the *chedi* in AD 704 – a date that would seem to owe more to poor maths or over-optimism than to historical veracity. However, it was reputedly restored by the ruler of Chiang Khong in 1881. The *viharn* sports some rather lurid murals. **Wat Phra Kaew**, a little further north, has two fine, red guardian lions at its entrance. Otherwise it is very ordinary, save for the *kutis* (small huts that serve as the monks' quarters) along the inside of the front wall, which look like a row of assorted Wendy houses, and the *nagas* which curl their way up the entrance to the *viharn*, on the far side of the building. Like Nong Khai and the other towns that line the Mekong in the northeastern region, *pla buk* catfish are caught here. It is sometimes possible to watch the fishermen catching a giant catfish on the riverbank to the south of town.

There are **hilltribe villages** within reach of Chiang Khong, but the trekking industry here is relatively undeveloped. Ask at the guesthouses to see if a guide is available. Tour operators cater mainly for those travelling on to Laos.

Mae Sai → *For listings, see pages 92-97.*

Marking Thailand's northernmost point, Mae Sai is a busy trading centre with Burma and has a rather clandestine and frenetic frontier atmosphere. The area around the bridge is the centre of activity, with stalls and shops selling gems and an array of Burmese and Chinese goods, from knitted hats and Burmese marionettes to antiques and animal skulls. With Burma and routes to Yunnan (China) opening up, the town is growing rapidly and the urban sprawl is spreading several kilometres south of the border. The main bus station is 5 km out of town, just off the main road running to Mae Chan and Chiang Rai. *Songthaews* and motorcycle taxis take passengers from town to the terminal and vice versa.

Wat Phrathat Doi Wao sits on a hill overlooking the town, off Phahonyothin Road, not far from the **Top North Hotel**. The wat is not particularly beautiful and was reputedly built in the mid-1960s in commemoration of a platoon of Burmese soldiers killed in action against a KMT (Kuomintang – the Chinese Republican Army) force.

Around Mae Sai

Luang Cave (Tham Luang) is an impressive cave with natural rock formations, 3 km off Route 110 to Chiang Rai, 7 km from town. After the initial large cavern, the passage narrows, over the course of 1 km, to a series of smaller chambers. Guides with lamps wait outside the cave to lead visitors – for a fee – through the system. To get there take a regular *songthaew* to the turn-off; ask for 'Tham loo-ang'.

Doi Tung is a 2000-m-high hill village, almost 50 km south of Mae Sai. The road snakes its way past Akha, Lahu and KMT villages, as well as former poppy fields, before reaching Wat Phrathat Doi Tung, some 24 km from the main road. The road is now surfaced to the summit, although it is still quite a stomach-churning journey and the road can deteriorate after heavy rain. The twin *chedis* on the summit are said to contain the left collarbone of the Buddha and to have been initially built by a king of Chiang Saen in the 10th century. The views from the wat are breathtaking. A few years ago the king's mother built a palace here, a vast Austrian/Thai chalet with fantastic views over what was, at the time of construction, a devastated and deforested landscape. (Depending on who you talk to, the culprits were either shifting cultivators growing opium or big business interests logging protected land.) With the king's mother's influence, the hills around the palace were reforested. These days Doi Tung is very popular with Thai day-trippers and there's an overpriced restaurant, some gardens and a café. To get there, travel south on Route 110 from Mae Sai for 22 km to Huai Klai and then turn off onto Route 1149. Or take a bus heading for Chiang Rai and ask to be let off in Ban Huai Klai, at the turn-off for Doi Tung. From there, *songthaews* run to Doi Tung. Now that the road is upgraded the *songthaew* service is rather more regular – but check on return journeys if you intend to make it back the same day; it is easiest to explore the area by rented motorbike.

Mae Salong (Santikhiri) → *For listings, see pages 92-97.*

Mae Salong is situated at an altitude of over 1200 m, close to the border with Burma. It is like a small pocket of China. After the Communist victory in China in 1949, remnants of the nationalist KMT (Kuomintang) sought refuge here and developed it as a base from which they would mount an invasion of China. This wish has long since faded into fantasy and the Thai authorities have attempted to integrate the exiled Chinese into the Thai mainstream. A paved road now leads to the town, which is now so easily accessible it has turned into one of Thailand's most popular weekend destinations, particularly with middle class Bangkokians who pack the place out from December to February. For New Year on 31 December, the place gets completely overrun with Thai tourists, and you'll be hard-pressed to find a room or any space to relax. Mae Salong is also an alternative trekking centre; it's easily possible to do day-hikes into the local Lisu and Akha villages from here. However, you should speak to locals about the current security situation before embarking on a trek, as the nearby Burmese border can lead to incursions by the rebel Wa Army, and the area is still a hive of drug-smuggling activity.

Despite the attempts to Thai-ify Mae Salong, it still feels Chinese. The hillsides, in season, are scattered with beautiful pink blossom, whilst Chinese herbs and vegetables are grown in the surrounding countryside and sold at the morning market. Many of the inhabitants still speak Chinese, Yunnanese food is sold on the streets, and there are glimpses of China everywhere. One of the reasons why Mae Salong has remained so distinctive is because a significant proportion of the KMT refugees who settled here became involved in opium production and trade. This put the inhabitants in conflict with the Thai authorities and created the conditions whereby they were excluded from mainstream Thai society. Mae Salong's remoteness – at least until recently – also isolated the town from intensive interaction with other areas of the country.

Tea growing has now become a massive industry in and around Mae Salong and the hills are filled with endless tea terraces while the village is now home to dozens of tea-houses. The local brew is subtle and tasty – the variety of Oolong is particularly good. Less nuanced and completely tasteless are attempts to build a weird **tea visitor centre** just outside of town. Here massive gold and silver concrete tea pots (soon to have fountains pouring from the spouts) sit beside giant Chinese dragons as surreal, gaudy evidence of someone with too much money and not enough sense.

The **morning market** is worth a visit for early risers (0530-0800), as this is where hilltribe people come to sell their produce. **Wat Santakhiri** is situated in a great position above the town. There's a long steep staircase just past the entrance to the **Mae Salong Resort**. Also worth a visit is the **Chinese Martyrs Memorial Museum** ① *look for the large gate about 1 km towards Tha Ton from the day market, daily 1000-1600, ฿50*, where the history of the KMT fighters who founded Mae Salong is mapped out. One room contains mini-red wooden plinths, each inscribed with the name of a fallen comrade.

The walk up to **General Tuan's tomb** on the road behind the **Khum Nai Phol Resort** is a pleasant diversion as well, with some friendly teashops and exhilarating views when you arrive. Tuan was the KMT leader who brought his men to Mae Salong, and he is still deeply revered locally.

Around Mae Salong

Thord Thai (Toerd Thai) is a small Shan village about 20 km north towards the Burmese border. It was here that Khun Sa, the legendary leader of the Shan state and notorious opium warlord, lived for a while. You can visit the house where he stayed and see a collection of photographs and other artefacts. There are a few signs for **Khun Sa House**, just ask around; there are no fixed opening hours, so aim for early afternoon when it's more likely the family across the road who hold the key will be there. To get to the village, you'll need to arrange your own transport or rent a motorbike. You can also walk there from Mae Salong in about three to four hours; ask at **Little Home** for directions. There is a guesthouse and some good places to eat in Thord Thai.

Trekking to **Akha** and other hilltribe villages is arranged by the **Little Home** or **Sinsane** guesthouses. The latter also organizes pony trekking to local hilltribe villages.

Chiang Saen and the Golden Triangle listings

For hotel and restaurant price codes and other relevant information, see pages 8-12.

🛏 Where to stay

Chiang Saen *p86*
$$$$-$$$ Siam Triangle Hotel, 267 Moo 9, T053-651115, www.siamtriangle.com. Brand new riverside hotel. Modern, contemporary rooms are best on the riverfront, where the large balconies have fantastic views. Dark woods and silk make up the pleasing rooms, complete with flat-screen TVs, Wi-Fi, a/c and en suite facilities. Nice bar, too.

$$$-$$ Chiang Saen River Hill Hotel, Phahonyothin Soi 2 (just inside the southern city walls), T053-650826, chiangsaen@ hotmail.com. The best hotel in town with 60 rooms over 4 storeys and a restaurant. It's nothing flash, but the management are friendly and the rooms are comfortable, with a/c, attached showers (very clean), minibar and TV.

$$$-$$ Pak-Ping-Rim-Khong, 484 Rimkhong Rd, Moo 2, T053-650151. Another new property for Chiang Saen, this time a purpose-built townhouse turned into a guesthouse on the main road by the river. The airy, well-lit rooms are finished off with relaxing dark hues, wooden features and tiled floors. All are en suite, and have a/c and Wi-Fi. There's also a small garden to sit in. Rooms at back are quieter. Recommended.

$ Sa Nae Charn Guest House, 641 Moo 2, T053-651138. Unkempt, though clean budget guesthouse that is perfect for those who are travelling on a shoestring. Basic rooms, and a friendly and knowledgeable English-speaking owner.

Sop Ruak *p88*
$$$$ Anantara Golden Triangle, 1 km north of Sop Ruak, T053-784084. Relatively peaceful location, with wonderful evening views. 'Traditional' architecture has been taken to the limit and it's a bit of a blot on the landscape for this timeless area of Thailand. However, the hotel is very well run with good service and facilities (including pool, tennis and squash courts, gymnasium, pétanque and sauna). It also runs an excellent Elephant Camp in conjunction with the Thai Elephant Conservation Centre near Lampang (see page 36).

$$$$-$$$ Imperial Golden Triangle Resort, 222 Golden Triangle, T053-784001, www.imperialhotels.com. It is rather a surprise coming upon a hotel like this in what should be a quiet corner of Thailand. 73 plush and tasteful a/c rooms, restaurant, pool. Well run and attractive but probably ill-conceived, as they seem to have difficulty filling the rooms. Large discounts available, especially in low season. Mainly aimed at package tourists.

$$$-$$ Baan Thai Resort, 526 Moo 1, www.sawasdeebaanthai.com, T053-652152. In a compound on the opposite side of the road to the river there are overpriced mini-wooden bungalows and good-value rooms in this tidy and welcoming establishment. The pleasing rooms all come a/c, en suite, TV and Wi-Fi as standard.

$$$-$$ The Mae Khong River Side,
587 Moo 1, T053-784198. Overpriced
though decent clean rooms with balconies
overlooking the Golden Triangle. They also
arrange boat trips. Good option if you want
a river view.

$$-$ Ban YooPenSuk, just off main road
away from river, T053-784339. Friendly,
eccentric owner. Budget bungalows –
all spotless, en suite and with a/c or fan –
and a pleasant, private garden.

Chiang Khong *p89, map p276*
There are dozens of guesthouses in Chiang
Khong, and many frequently change name
and owners.
$$$-$$ Baan Golden Triangle, on top of
a hill to the north of town, T053-791350.
This is a stab at a 'back-to-nature' resort,
with wooden bungalows, garden and cart
wheels. The rooms are fine, with attached
bathrooms and hot water. Great views, too,
over a tiny rice valley to the Mekong and Laos.
$$$-$$ Ruan Thai Sophaphan Resort,
Tambon Wiang Rd, T053-791023. Big wooden
house with a large raised veranda. Rooms are
large and clean with en suite and hot water.
The upstairs rooms are better and have
more natural light. There are also bungalows
for 2-4 people. Good river views, very
friendly, restaurant, self-service drinks, price
negotiable out of season. Recommended.
$$-$ Bamboo Riverside, Sai Khlang Rd,
T053-791621. Generally a higher standard
of huts to the rest of the places in this
category. Rooms have balconies overlooking
the river, with clean, hot showers. Friendly
owners speak good English and are full
of information. The restaurant has superb
views over the river to Laos and serves great
Mexican food and freshly baked bread.
$$-$ Ban Tam Mi La, 8/1 Sai Klang Rd,
down a side street (northern end of town),
T053-791234. Set in an attractive rambling
garden along the riverside. Cheaper rooms
are very basic with mosquito net and shared
bathroom; more expensive rooms have
private bathrooms; bungalows have river

views. Restaurant serves good food. Friendly
and helpful, although some recent visitors
have said that it is overpriced.
$$-$ Namkhong Guesthouse & Resort,
94/2 Moo2, T053-791055. There are some
real bargains to be had at this well-known
sprawling guesthouse. Nice wooden rooms
come complete with some decorative
touches, a/c or fan. There's also a pool,
although even guests have to pay a small
fee to use it. Unfortunately, it's all let down
by indifferent service.
$ Green Inn, 89/4 Moo2, T053-791009.
With a central location on the main road,
this mini-hotel has good, clean rooms,
some with a/c, hot water en suite facilities
and TVs. The cheaper rooms are dark but
spotless, with shared bathrooms.
$ Green Tree Guesthouse, Sai Khlang Rd
(in front of the **Namkhong Riverside**),
T08-9952 1730 (mob), www.greentreegh.
blogspot.com. Pleasant yet basic rooms
with shared hot-water showers in a Lanna-
style old house, plus 3 A-frame bungalows
out back. Nice shady restaurant, free
Wi-Fi and a friendly owner with exceptional
English. Lots of information; tours available.
Recommended.
$ Portside, 546 Moo 1, Tambon Wiang Rd,
T053-655238. Guesthouse right next to the
port/immigration for crossing into Laos. The
airy rooms on the upper floors are the best,
with a/c or fan, TV and hot water en suite.
It's spotless throughout, with a big roof
terrace, where the owners put up tents to
accommodate extra guests. Free Wi-Fi.

Mae Sai *p90*
Mae Sai's accommodation is now squarely
aimed at business people who've come
here to trade. Standards and prices have
risen accordingly.
$$$$-$$ Wang Thong, 299 Phahonyothin
Rd, T053-733388. Set back from the road in
the centre of town, this new high-rise hotel
gets rather overrun by tour groups. 150 small
a/c rooms with rather over-the-top decor,
restaurant and pool. Low-season discounts.

$$$-$$ Afterglow Hostel, 139/5 Moo 4 Wiang Phang Kham, T053-734188, www.afterglowhostel.com. Reminiscent of Bangkok's new wave of flashpacker digs, this spacious hostel has a big reception and lounge area, plus clean, funky rooms pairing exposed concrete with primary colours. A/c, TV.

$$$-$$ Chour Place, 114 Phaholyothin Rd, on the main road about 1 km from the border, T053-733787, www.chourplace.com. Slightly oddball exterior reveals a pleasant-enough contemporary Thai hotel with all the mod-cons you'd expect (TVs, a/c, Wi-Fi, etc).

$$$-$$ Maekhong Delta Boutique Hotel, 230/9 Phaholyothin Rd, about 1.5 km from the border, T053-642517, www.maekhong hotel.com. Welcoming, with an array of rooms and prices. Most rooms come with either tiled or wooden floors, while the pick are at the back and have balconies as well.

$$$-$$ Piyaporn Place Hotel, 77/1 Phaholyothin Rd, about 600 m from the border, T053-734511, www.piyaporn-place.com. This is not a bad option. Rooms are fairly unmemorable, but are clean, with wooden floors, TVs, en suite bathrooms and a/c. Those on the upper floors have nice views.

$$-$ Yeesun Hotel, 816/13 Sawlongchong Rd, T053-733455. Decent small hotel aimed mainly at Thais but still a good deal. Rooms are a/c, with hot showers and cable TV.

$ Littlebear House, 129/10 Soi-Tessabarn-6, 800 m from the border, T053-640933, www.littlebear-house.com. Down a small soi off the main road, this funky little Thai-owned guesthouse has phenomenally cheap, clean and adequate rooms with fan or a/c. There's a small bar attached, with Wi-Fi.

$ S House, 384 Sailomjoy Rd, T053-733811, www.s-house-hotel-maesai.com. Set in the middle of the riverside market, S-House has plenty of atmosphere and, with its well-decorated but basic en suite rooms, with either a/c or fan, it's one of the best budget options in town. Get rooms on the top floor for more light/views.

Mae Salong (Santikhiri) *p91*

There's now an excellent range of places to stay in Mae Salong, making it a great base to explore the local hills. Discounts can be negotiated in the low season.

$$$$-$$ Mae Salong Flower Hills Resort, T053-765496, www.maesalong flowerhills.com. This sprawling hillside resort looks out of place, with its immaculately coiffeured lawns and pruned topiary, but it does offer surprisingly good value and a friendly welcome. The a/c bungalows have pretty views down across tea terraces, as does the big restaurant. There's even a pool. Downside? It's a tad soulless.

$$$-$$ Khum Nai Phol Resort, 58 Moo 1, T053-765 001, www.khumnaipholresort.com. Easy-to-find option opposite the day market and a mini-mart. Simple wood/bamboo weave bungalows sit uphill from reception above rows of tea terraces. Decor is dowdy, but the balconies are a good spot to listen to the tinny sounds of Chinese karaoke echoing across the hills in the evenings. Restaurant is open later than most, serving Thai and Yunnanese. Should you need to check your email, the friendly Thai owner might let you use her laptop.

$$$-$$ Osman House (Thai sign only), opposite **Sweet Mae Salong** café, T053-0765271. Beautiful wooden rooms, complete with huge bay windows, gorgeous silk-finished furnishings, flat-screen TVs and private en suite facilities, are a bit let down by the location on the main road, which can get incredibly noisy early in the morning. Try to get a room at the back.

$$ Mae Salong Resort, T053-765014. Individual though basic bungalows are set in a small village of their own, on a pine-covered hill. There's a Chinese/Thai restaurant and several stalls and shops that sell trinkets and Chinese products (such as tea).

$$-$ Baan See See, just up the hill from **Little Home**, T053-765053, www.baansee see.com. 2-room concrete bungalows, all with fan and en suite bathrooms, are spread over this tiny hillside compound. The owners are very friendly.

$$-$ Little Home Guesthouse, 31 Moo 1 (next to Shin Sane), T053-765389, www.maesalonglittlehome.com. One of the friendliest and best-run small guesthouses in this part of the north. The owner, Somboon – an ex child soldier with the KMT – and his family really go out of their way to be hospitable. There are basic, spotless rooms in the teak house at the front and a couple of bungalows for rent at the back. They also serve food, drinks and have internet access. Highly recommended.

$ Akha Guesthouse, next door to Sinsane. Clean, basic, big rooms with shared bathrooms. A bit noisy but friendly management.

$ Fun Fun Inn, behind the 7-11, T053-765168, www.maesalongfunfuninn.com. Very tidy and neat little guesthouse in a quiet location in the middle of Mae Salong. Rooms come with stone floors and wooden furnishings, TVs, fans and en suite bathrooms. Recommended.

$ Jabusee Homestay, small village a few kilometres from Mae Salong, T053-765129/T08-1021 3992. A Lahu village just outside Mae Salong provides the most basic accommodation in simple huts as part of an excellent and highly recommended homestay programme. Stay with the family and take part in numerous activities, such as weaving. They also offer food.

$ Saeng Aroon Hotel, opposite Little Home, T053-765029. With its eccentric yet captivatingly friendly owners, Saeng Aroon is a small slice of Yunnan China in north Thailand. The rooms have imported chintzy Chinese furniture and tiled floors, but are spotless; those at the back on the upper floors have fine views. A Footprint favourite. Recommended.

$ Sinsane. Mae Salong's oldest hostelry is in an original wooden building with plenty of atmosphere. The rooms are basic but more than adequate, and there are several stand-alone bungalows around the back. Fan

only, shared facilities in the cheaper rooms. Friendly atmosphere and the food is good. The owner can arrange pony treks.

Thord Thai *p91*

$ Rimtaan Guest House, on main road from Mae Salong, T053-730209. This is the only place in Thord Thai village that's worth staying in. Nice fan bungalows, with en suite facilities, are set-up in pretty gardens next to a small river. Friendly if a little soporific service. Recommended.

⦿ Restaurants

Chiang Saen *p86*
The areas out of town towards Sop Ruak and the Golden Triangle have better riverside restaurants selling good Thai food, eg **Rim Khong** (2 km north of the city walls) and the **Mekong River Banks** (3 km).

$ Danang Vietnam Kitchen, Rimkhong Rd, near the **Chiang Saen Guesthouse**. Good Vietnamese food and noodles.

$ Nameless restaurant, corner of Rob Wiang and Phahonyothin roads. Clean and well-run place serving simple dishes, coffee, ice cream, etc.

$ Riverside, close to the **Chiang Saen Guesthouse**. Probably the best restaurant in town.

Foodstalls
There are a number of cheap *kwaytio* stalls along the riverbank and on Phahonyothin Rd.

Chiang Khong *p89*
In town, along the main road, there are a number of noodle and rice stalls. The more interesting places are along the river road, or down one of the *sois* leading to the Mekong.

$$ Bamboo Riverside Guesthouse, Sai Khlang Rd (see Where to stay, above). Great views over the Mekong to Laos and excellent Mexican food. Recommended.

$$ Nong Kwan, Sai Khlang Rd. Serves great Thai food at reasonable prices. The chicken and cashew dishes are recommended.

$$ Ruan Thai Sophaphan Resort, see Where to stay, above. Very comfortable with wicker chairs, cold beer, a great view and good food.
$ Rimkhong, in the centre, and **Rim Naam**, next door, are good value but the fish dishes are rather limited and hardly memorable.

Mae Sai *p90*
Restaurants in Mae Sai tend to be serious eating establishments with little character. There are numerous places along Phahonyothin Rd and the market area is good for cheaper stall food. Most guesthouses have restaurants serving Thai food. You'll find a run of small shophouses selling excellent Chinese-style roast port and rice on the road to Chiang Rai about 2 km from the border.
$$ Daw Restaurant (Thai sign), Sailomjoy Rd. Serves up delicious Thai grub. Highly recommended.

Mae Salong (Santikhiri) *p91*
Mae Salong is a good place to eat Yunnanese food, and there are some great noodle shops around the village. Try the one on the T-junction at the end of the morning market, or the one about 100 m down the main road from the **7-11**. The bakery just down the hill from **Sinsane** also serves great Yunnanese fried noodles.
$$ Sweet Mae Salong. An excellent café serving probably the best chocolate brownies in the whole country. The friendly owners speak great English and offer a range of Thai/ Western food and superb coffee. It's a little pricey but the quality/ value is very high, and there's free internet for customers. There's a great little balcony overlooking the hills and magazines to browse. Recommended.
$ Little Home Guesthouse, see Where to stay, above. Great noodle and Thai dishes.
$ Salima Restaurant, 300 m past **Sinsane** guesthouse (see Where to stay, above). This Muslim restaurant is probably the best place to eat in town. The owners are very friendly,

speak almost no English and are slightly eccentric. Try the Chinese bun with beef curry. Memorable and recommended.

Thord Thai *p91*
$ Ting Ting, next to **Rimtaan Guesthouse** on main road from Mae Salong. The constant aroma of grilled pork and chicken should attract you here. Excellent Shan and Thai food on sale from the very friendly Shan proprietors. Recommended.

○ Shopping

Mae Sai *p90*
Most people come to Mae Sai for the shopping, and the vast market here is now one of the most enthralling in Thailand. There are scores of stalls and shops selling Burmese, Chinese, Lao and Thai goods. The Burmese products are the most diverse and the best buys: puppets, cheroots, gemstones, 'antiques' and lacquerware.

Mae Salong (Santikhiri) *p91*
There's not a lot to buy in Mae Salong but there are a lot of tea shops selling the wonderful local oolong and green teas, plus pretty Chinese tea sets. Many of these places also stock a huge variety of very tasty dried fruit. Probably the best are the 10 varieties of dried cherries, all sourced locally. Visiting these places for tea tasting is recommended, however, if you just expect repeated handouts, the locals will soon get annoyed.

○ What to do

Chiang Khong *p89*
Tour operators
There are a growing number of tour companies in Chiang Khong. **Ann Tour**, 6/1 Sai Klang Rd, T053-791218, is recommended. **Chiang Khong Tour** and **Nam Khong Travel**, north of town, by the pier, get most of their business arranging visas for Laos. For further information on visas, see page 16.

Mae Salong (Santikhiri) *p91*

Somboon at Little Home Guesthouse (see Where to stay, above) can help arrange tours or put you in contact with the right people. He also has motorbikes for hire and can arrange private transfers to and from Chiang Rai and other destinations. Sinsane (see Where to stay, above) arranges pony trekking from ฿500 per person.

◎ Transport

Chiang Saen *p86*
Bus

There are regular connections with Chiang Rai (1 hr 20 mins), Mae Sai (1 hr) and Chiang Khong (2 hrs).

Sop Ruak *p88*
Songthaew

Regular connections with Mae Sai (40 mins) and Chiang Saen (10 mins, ฿10). Just flag one down on the road – they run through Sop Ruak about every 40 mins.

Chiang Khong *p89*
Bus

There are hourly connections with Chiang Rai (3 hrs). A/c and non-a/c connections with Bangkok and Chiang Mai (6½ hrs), as well as Lampang and Phayao. A/c buses leave from the office on the main road near Wat Phra Kaew. Non-a/c buses depart from the bus station, just over the Huai Sob Som on the south edge of town. Non-a/c buses for Chiang Saen leave from 0600, and take the attractive river road following the Mekong and the Thai-Lao border (2 hrs).

Songthaew

Regular connections with Chiang Saen and from there on to Sop Ruak, Mae Sai and Chiang Rai. *Songthaews* leave from opposite the army post next to the post office, but can be flagged down as they make their way north through Chiang Khong.

Mae Sai *p90*
Bus

Regular connections with Bangkok's Northern bus terminal (13-15 hrs), Chiang Mai (5 hrs), Chiang Rai (1 hr 20 mins), and Mae Chan (45 mins-1½ hrs).

Songthaew

Connections with Chiang Saen, Sop Ruak and the Golden Triangle, every 30-40 mins. *Songthaews* leave from Phahonyothin Rd, near the centre of town. *Songthaews* for Mae Chan and Chiang Rai also leave from town, saving a journey out to the bus terminal.

Mae Salong (Santikhiri) *p91*
Songthaew

To get to Mae Salong from Chiang Rai take the Mae Sai-bound bus and get off at Mae Chan. From there, *songthaews* run 6 times daily 0600-1400 (1½ hrs) with the same number in the opposite direction. From Mae Salong to Tha Thon there are 5 *songthaews* a day (2 hrs) 0730-1530. Little Home Guesthouse has the full timetable.

Phrae, Nan and the Eastern Highlands

The Eastern Highlands, an area of outstanding natural beauty with a relaxed vibe and an intriguing history, is still off the main tourist and backpacker routes. The lack of development adds to its charm: the area's burgeoning tourist industry is easily integrated into a genuine slice of Thai rural life. The provincial capital, Phrae, is an attractive and friendly town with good accommodation and restaurants, situated in a narrow rice valley on the banks of the Mae Yom River, flanked by mountains to the east and west. Nan is a province to be explored for its natural beauty. Fertile valleys are chequered with paddy fields, teak plantations, hilltribes and fast-flowing rivers. It was not until 1931 that the central authorities managed to overcome the area's inaccessibility and bring Nan under Bangkok's direct control. Ever since then, there have been periods – most recently in the 1970s when Communist insurgency was a problem – when the army and police have treated the province as a no-go area, and it still exudes an atmosphere of other-worldliness and isolation. The area also boasts rarely visited national parks, some of the finest forest in the country, weaving villages and excellent hill treks. In the last few years, travel through Phrae and Nan has become an increasingly feasible alternative route to Laos, although, it t is still rarely used because onward travel on the Laos side of the border is not so easy. A through road to Luang Prabang is rumoured to be on the cards but, at the time of writing, this was still on the drawing board.

Phrae → *For listings, see pages 102-105.*

Phrae was founded in the 12th century – when it was known as Wiang Kosai or Silk Cloth City – and is one of the oldest cities in Thailand. It still has its own 'royal' family and was an independent Thai *muang* (city state) until the early 16th century, when it was captured by an army from Ayutthaya. When Ayutthaya's power began to wane in the 18th century, Phrae – like many other northern principalities – came under the sway of the Burmese. It was finally incorporated into the Siamese state in the 19th century.

Phrae's ancient roots can still be seen in the city walls and moat, which separate the old city from the new commercial centre. On Charoen Muang Road, there are a handful of attractive wooden Chinese shophouses, although the scourge of uncontrolled development is gradually gnawing away at the remnants of old Phrae.

Arriving in Phrae

Phrae is not a large place and the town is pleasant enough to stroll around. The main bus terminal is a 15-minute walk from most of the accommodation. It's 7 km northeast of the centre off Yantaeakitkoson Road, opposite the Maeyom Palace Hotel. The airport is 7 km southeast of town. The nearest train station to Phrae is at Den Chai, 24 km southwest of town. Regular buses and *songthaews* run from the train station into town.

Places in Phrae

During World War Two, Thailand became an ally of Nazi Germany and the Japanese; in fact, many of Thailand's leading military and political figures in the late 20th century had fought against the Allies. Yet a resistance movement of sorts did exist. Known as the Seri or 'Free' Thai, it had Thammasat University founder and leading Thai social democrat, Pridi Banomyong, as its leader and much of its activity was centred in Phrae. The former Seri Thai HQ is sited in a beautiful old school building just behind the **Paradorn Hotel**. It is now the **Seri Thai Museum** ⓘ *daily 1000-1700, free*, one of the north's best little museums. It charts the Seri Thai's resistance to the Japanese invaders, with plenty of information in English, including a thank you letter from George W Bush. Sadly, the memory of the Seri Thai is largely forgotten in Thailand today.

The Burmese-style **Wat Chom Sawan** ⓘ *on the edge of town, 1 km northeast of the centre, on the road to Nan, admission by donation*, was commissioned by Rama V (1868-1910) and designed by a Burmese architect. Like most Burmese (Thai Yai) wats, the *bot* and *viharn* are consolidated in one elaborate, multi-roofed towering structure, with verandas and side rooms. It has survived relatively unscathed; the wooden roof tiles have not been replaced by corrugated iron, and the rich original interior decoration of mirror tiles upon a deep red ground is also intact. Ask one of the monks to point out the rare Buddhist texts carved on sheets of ivory, and the bamboo and gold Buddha 'basket'.

Wat Luang ⓘ *admission by donation*, is a few minutes' walk from Wat Sri Chum, near the city wall and moat. The wat was founded in the 12th century, although continuous renovation and expansion has obscured its ancient origins. The wat also supports an impressive museum which houses valuable Buddha images, swords, coins, burial caskets, Buddhist texts, old photographs (one of a decapitation), betel boxes and jewellery. An old northern house, with all the accessories of traditional life, is also part of the collection. Finally, the wat is also notable for its fine well pavilion on the west wall and the individual monk's *kutis*, or cells, like small bungalows, along the south wall.

Nan → *For listings, see pages 102-105.*

A charming, friendly town with a historical ambience, Nan occupies a small valley in the far north of the Eastern Highlands – about 50 km from the border with Laos. The airport is on the northern edge of town (5 km from the centre). It is thought the earliest settlers arrived from Laos in 1282, establishing a town 70 km north of Nan. According to legend, the Buddha himself was trekking here, picking out auspicious sites for wats, over 2500 years ago. The 13th-century inscriptions of King Ramkhamhaeng of Sukhothai named Nan as one of the *muang* whose 'submission he received', although it would be more accurate to view the royal house of Nan ruling autonomously until the 15th century, when Lanna established suzerainty over Nan. Even then, the turbulent politics of the area, with the Burmese, Lao, Siamese and the *muang* of the area all vying with one another, coupled with Nan's location, afforded it considerable independence. These days, Nan is having something of a renaissance and has become a popular destination for wealthy Bangkok hipsters.

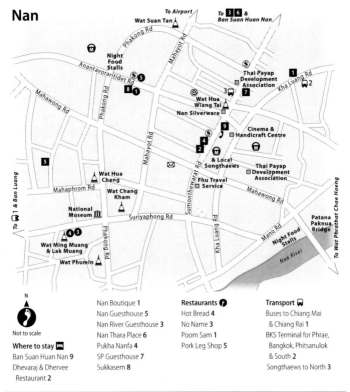

Nan

N

Not to scale

Where to stay 🛏
Ban Suan Huan Nan 9
Dhevaraj & Dhervee
Restaurant 2
Nan Boutique 1
Nan Guesthouse 5
Nan River Guesthouse 3
Nan Thara Place 6
Pukha Nanfa 4
SP Guesthouse 7
Sukkasem 8

Restaurants 🍴
Hot Bread 4
No Name 3
Poom Sam 1
Pork Leg Shop 5

Transport 🚌
Buses to Chiang Mai
& Chiang Rai 1
BKS Terminal for Phrae,
Bangkok, Phitsanulok
& South 2
Songthaews to North 3

Places in Nan

The **National Museum** ① *Phakong Rd, Wed-Sun 0900-1600, ฿30*, once the home of the Nan royal family, houses an impressive collection, including beautiful wood and bronze Buddha images, ceramics, textiles, jewellery and musical instruments. There's a decent ethnographic display offering an insight into the lives of the local ethnic groups and a collection of stone-age tools. On the second floor, protected in a steel cage, is a 97-cm-long black elephant tusk that once belonged to the Nan royal family and is reputed to have magic powers. This is a great little museum and well worth a visit; exhibits are well displayed with English explanations throughout.

Just opposite the National Museum is **Wat Phumin** ① *Phakong Rd*. Built in 1596 it was restored between 1865 and 1873. The cruciform *bot-cum-viharn* is supported by the coils of two magnificent *nagas* (mythical serpents). The head forms the buttress of the north entrance, and the tail the south. Inside, there are some of the finest murals to be found in the north. Painted at the end of the 19th century – probably in 1894 – they depict the tale of the Sihanadajataka, but also illustrate aspects of northern Thai life: hunting, weaving, lovers, musicians, elephants, courtiers, a starving *farang* clasping a tool for pre-masticating food (eastern wall, top) and people with over-sized testicles. The naive style of the murals – large areas of empty space, figures of various sizes – distinguish them from the sophisticated art of Bangkok.

Wat Chang Kham, on the diagonally opposite corner to Wat Phumin, features a *chedi* supported by elephant buttresses (caryatids), similar to those at Sukhothai. The *viharn* was built in 1547 and contains three Sukhothai-style Buddha images: two walking and one standing. There's a large seminary here and the temple compound is often filled with dozens of friendly, shaven-headed novices.

Wat Ming Muang ① *Suriyaphong Rd*, contains the city of Nan's **lak muang** (city pillar), liberally draped in garlands. Wat Hua Chang, on the corner of Phakong and Mahaphrom roads, features a two-storey stone and wood *tripitaka*, or scripture, library, a square-based *chedi* with four Buddhas in raised niches and a fine *bot* (with *bai sema*). Gaudy **Wat Hua Wiang Tai** ① *Sumonthewarat Rd, just north of Anantavoraritdet Rd*, has *nagas* running along the top of the surrounding wall and bright murals painted on the exterior of the *viharn*. Other wats in the town include **Wat Suan Tan**, in Tambon Nai Wiang, which has a *prang* – unusual for the area – and a 15th-century bronze Buddha image named Phra Chao Thong Thit. A fireworks display takes place at the wat during **Songkran**.

Around Nan

Wat Phrathat Chae Haeng, 3 km southeast of town across the Nan River, is a 30-minute walk (or rent a bicycle or motorbike). Built in 1355, the 55-m-high, gold-sheeted *chedi* is Lao in style, and the *bot* has an interesting multi-tiered roof. A fair with fireworks and processions is held here on the full moon day of the first lunar month). Also notable are the fine pair of *nagas* that form the balustrade of the approach stairway to the monastery.

Tha Wang Pha, 40 km to the north of Nan on Route 1080, is the district capital and famous for its Tai Lue weaving. The Tai Lue were forced out of Yunnan in southern China by King Rama I (1782-1809); they settled in Nan province, turned to farming and are now peacefully assimilated into the Thai population. However, they still retain some cultural distinctiveness: the skilled weavers wear a tubular *pha sin* of bright stripes and a black jacket, decorated with multicoloured embroidered stripes and silver jewellery. Tai Lue textiles and jewellery are available in town. To get to Tha Wang Pha from Nan, take a regular local bus or *songthaew* from the stand on Sumonthewarat Road, just north of Anantavoraritdet Road.

Located 70 km north of Nan, **Doi Phu Kha National Park** is one of northern Thailands largest and newest protected areas, covering more than 1700 sq km. The mountainous park offers good trekking and is named after a 1980-m peak, which offers exhilarating views from its peak. The limestone mountain ranges also harbour an abundance of waterfalls, caves, crags and grottoes, while the deciduous and evergreen forest provides a home for a range of hilltribes and various rare and near extinct flora, notably the pink-flowered Chomphu Phukha (*Bretschneidera ninensis hems 1*). Check at Park HQ for details on trekking. The best time to visit is between November and February, but it is cold at this time of year, so take warm clothes. The rainy season is May to October. To get to the park, catch a bus to **Pua** (one hour from Nan), which also makes a great base from which to explore the park; from Pua, *songthaews* run from 0800 to 1200 up to the Park HQ (they can be chartered at other times).

Phrae, Nan and the Eastern Highlands listings

For hotel and restaurant price codes and other relevant information, see pages 8-12.

☞ Where to stay

Phrae *p99*

$$$-$$ Maeyom Palace, 1 km from the centre, 81/6 Yantarakitkoson Rd, T054-521028. The best hotel in town, with large rooms, professional service, a/c, restaurant and pool (non-guests ฿45). Organizes tours to hilltribe villages and home industries. Discounts available, especially in low season. Bikes for hire (฿100 per day).

$$-$ Pharadorn, 177 Yantarakitkoson Rd, T054-511540. Rooms are spacious and clean, a/c rooms benefit from carpets and hot water. Some a/c, restaurant, karaoke bar. Good value, friendly, with Wi-Fi and breakfast.

$$-$ Thepvong Place Hotel, 346/2 Chaloenmuang Rd, T054-532428, www.thepvongplace.com. Fairly basic, though adequate a/c and fan rooms (all en suite) in this 4-storey building set down a quiet soi. The staff are friendly and speak some English.

Nan *p100, map p100*

$$$$-$$$ Pukha Nanfa Hotel, 369 Sumondevaraj Rd, T054-771111, www.pukhananfahotel.co.th. In 2009 the run-down 100-year-old Nanfa Hotel was bought and converted into Nan's most luxurious accommodation. The owners have done a fine job, maintaining nearly all of the original teak fittings and creating several gorgeous and sumptuous rooms, with silks, local artefacts and designer touches. The rooms are on the small side but this is still a fantastic property if you can afford the price tag. Wi-Fi, flat-screen TVs, en suite facilities and a nice relaxing private library complete the appeal.

$$$$-$$$ Nan Boutique Hotel, 1/11 Khaluang Rd, T054-775532, www.tazshotels.com. Contemporary Thai boutique resort with private gardens and spacious, well-lit en suite rooms with a/c, TV, free Wi-Fi and balconies. They also offer free airport transfers and bicycles. Decent café and restaurant attached.

$$$-$$ Ban Suan Huan Nan, 38/23 Premprisa Rd, T054-711864. Brand new small hotel, built at the end of a quiet soi in its own grounds. Rooms are large, with some artistic decorations, tiled floors, balconies, Wi-Fi, TVs, a/c and bathrooms.

$$$-$ Dhevaraj (pronounced – *thewarat*), 445 Sumonthewarat Rd, T054-757577. Range of good, if bland, hotel rooms, some a/c, some fan, all en suite. Clean and well run, pool, spa and excellent restaurant. Recommended.

$$-$ Nan Guesthouse, 57/16 Mahaphrom Rd, T054-771849. Nice guesthouse in quiet backstreet. More expensive rooms are en suite. Clean, friendly. Recommended.

$$-$ Nan River Guesthouse, 1 Mano Rd, T08-96359375. Friendly little guesthouse run by the same female couple who own Hot Bread (see Restaurants, below). Small, basic rooms in a town villa in a very quiet part of Nan, away from the centre. All have shared facilities and are fan-only. There are plenty of communal spaces: garden, living room and even a kitchen. Bicycles available, and owners will collect you from the bus station/airport or transfer you from Hot Bread. Recommended.

$$-$ Nan Thara Place, 72 Jaipahsuk Rd, T054-750678, www.nantharaplace.com. Set a little bit outside the town centre, this family-run guesthouse is a real bargain. The rooms are spotless, tiled, airy and open onto views of the distant hills. TV, Wi-Fi, en suite facilities and a very friendly welcome complete the picture. You'll probably need at least a bicycle if you plan to stay here. Recommended.

$$-$ SP Guest House, 231-233 Sumonthewarat Rd. T054-774897. A family-run guesthouse set around a small courtyard in a great central location. The newer and pricier rooms, with a/c, TV and hot showers, represent the best value.

$$-$ Sukkasem Hotel, 119-121 Anantavoraritidet Rd, T054-772555. With its clean, bright wooden and tiled rooms, this recently renovated hotels is one of the best deals in Nan. Upstairs rooms at the back have the best light and views. All with a/c, Wi-Fi and en suite bathrooms. Recommended.

Around Nan *p101*
Doi Phu Kha National Park
2 government houses rent out rooms in the park when officials are not staying. Pay by donation. There are also 14 bungalows with shared toilets and 2 campsites; see www.dnp.go.th for more details.

$$-$ Green Hill Resort, down road behind 7-11 in Pua, T054-791111, www.greenhill pua.com. Cheap and cheerful little operation that provides a perfect staging post if you

want to explore Doi Phu Kha. Friendly owners provide clean rooms, with tiled floors, hot showers, TV, Wi-Fi and balconies with nice views.

Restaurants

Phrae *p99*
There is a series of good little restaurants and foodstalls stretching along Charoen Muang and Robmuang roads and there are several bars on Rachdamnern Rd.

$$ Krua Yom Hom, Maeyom Palace Hotel, Yantarakitkoson Rd. Expensive Thai, Chinese and European food, but the live music and seafood barbecue in the evening makes it worth it.

$ Arun Chai, Charoen Muang Rd. Good food.

$ Good Time, Yantarakitkoson Rd. Daily 0900-1800. Cafe-cum-Thai eatery, with a/c and Wi-Fi. Good cake, coffee, ice cream and Thai dishes. Recommended.

Nan *p100, map p100*
$$-$ Poom Sam, Anantavoraritidet Rd. Daily 1100-late. One of Nan's most famous restaurants; their massaman curry is a national prize-winning dish and is one of Nan's must-eats. Recommended.

$ Dhervee, Dhevaraj Hotel, see Where to stay, above. Serves up a large range of excellent Thai food. It also has a tasty lunchtime buffet (daily 1100-1400) for ฿59, including coffee, soft drinks and dessert – a great deal for the quality. Recommended.

$ Hot Bread, 38/2 Suriyaphong Rd. Good veggie menu, freshly baked bread, cookies, great coffee and friendly English-speaking owner. Also rent bicycles. Recommended.

$ Pork Leg Shop, Anantavoraritidet Rd, opposite Poom Sam. 1600ish-late. Great little khao kah moo (pork leg over rice) place popular with locals. Recommended.

$ Pupaiyak Coffee Shop, Robmuang Rd. Daily 0700-1900. Serves locally grown coffee and nice cakes and ice cream. Also sells some locally made products.

$ Restaurant (no name) 38/1 Suriyaphong Rd (next to Hot Bread). Excellent spicy *kwaytio khao soi* (egg noodles in curry broth) and home-made *moo daeng* (BBQ pork) over rice. They sell out quickly so get here before 1200. Recommended.

Foodstalls

There is a small night market at the intersection of Phakong and Anantavoraritidet roads, lots of decent noodle shops along Sumonthewarat Rd and an excellent daytime food market just opposite the **Dhevaraj Hotel** (see Where to stay, above). You'll also find an array of foodstalls in the evening just by the Patana Pakaua Bridge. There are now an array of trendy coffee shops aimed at Bangkok hipsters down Sumonthewarat Rd.

✸ Festivals

Nan *p100, map p100*
Mid Oct-mid Nov Boat races, at the end of the Buddhist Lent. These races are thought to have started about a century ago, when they were part of the Songkran celebrations. The boats are hollowed-out logs, painted in bright designs. There is a lively fair in the weeks before (and during) the races.

◎ Shopping

Phrae *p99*
Morhom Mae Nuu, 60-62 Charoen Muang Rd. Phrae is a centre of *morhom* production – the traditional blue garb of the northern farmer. Available all over town, but **Morhom Mae Nuu** is recommended. A simple tunic costs ฿60-100.

Nan *p100, map p100*
Nan Silverware, corner of Sumonthewarat and Anantavoraritidet roads, for locally produced jewellery.
Nara Department store, Sumonthewarat Rd, north of intersection with Anantaroraritidet Rd.

◎ What to do

Nan *p100, map p100*
Tour operators
Fhu Travel Service, 453/4 Sumonthewarat Rd, T054-710636. The best tour company in town. Mr Fhu rents out bicycles and motorbikes and arranges treks to see local hilltribes, the Doi Phu Kha National Park, provincial sites and boat tours up the Nan River. Prices from ฿600 per day upwards – given the quality of the service provided this is good value for money.

The **Dhevaraj, Nan Guesthouse, Doi Phukha** and **Nanfa** also organize tours.

⊖ Transport

Phrae *p99*
Air
3 flights a week to and from **Bangkok**'s Don Muang airport with **Nok Air** (www.nokair.com).

Bus
Regular connections with **Bangkok**'s Northern bus terminal (8¼ hrs), **Uttaradit**, **Chiang Mai** and other towns in the north (hourly connections with Nan, 2-2½ hrs). A/c tour buses for **Bangkok** leave from **Phrae Tour**'s offices at 141/6 Yantarakitkoson Rd at 2030 and 2100.

Songthaew
Songthaew is the main form of local transport. *Songthaews* running north to **Song** and **Rong Kwang** leave from outside the Piriyalai School on Yantarakitkoson Rd; those running south to **Den Chai** (for the nearest train station) depart from Yantarakitkoson Rd near the intersection with Muang Hit Rd (by the petrol station).

Train
The nearest train station to Phrae is at **Den Chai**, 24 km southwest of town. Connections south to **Bangkok** (8½ hrs) and north to

Chiang Mai (4½ hrs). To get to Den Chai, pick up a bus on Yantarakitkoson Rd near the intersection with Muang Hit Rd (by the petrol station).

Nan *p100, map p100*
Air
Daily flights to **Bangkok**'s Don Muang airport with **Nok Air** (www.nokair.com). **Kan Air** are currently operating a 4 times a week flight to/from **Chiang Mai** but it is unclear how long this will continue (www.kanairlines.com).

Bicycle and motorbike
Hire is available from **Fhu Travel Service**, **Oversea Shop**, **Nan** and **Hot Bread**.

Bus
Nan has 2 bus terminals. Buses for towns to the north and west, including **Chiang Rai**, **Chiang Mai** (6½ hrs, ฿117), **Lamphun**, **Lampang**, **Phrae** and **Den Chai**, leave from the station off Anantavoraritdet Rd about 1 km west of the town centre. Buses running north to **Chiang Rai** take 2 routes: either a trip west and northwest on routes 1091 and 1251 to Phayao and then north to Chiang Rai, or by first running south to Phrae and then north to Phayao and Chiang Rai.

Buses serving destinations to the south, including **Bangkok**'s Northern bus terminal (9½-10 hrs), **Phitsanulok**, **Uttaradit**, **Nakhon Sawan**, **Kamphaeng Phet** and **Sukhothai**, leave from the BKS terminal, 500 m to the north of the city centre on Kha Luang Rd. VIP and a/c buses go to major destinations. Bus times and costs are displayed on boards at the **Nan** and **Doi Phukha** guesthouses. The information officers at the terminals speak English.

Contents

Footnotes

Useful words and phrases

Thai is a tonal language with five tones: mid tone (no mark), high tone (´), low tone (`), falling tone (ˆ), and rising tone (ˇ). Tones are used to distinguish between words which are otherwise the same. For example, 'see' pronounced with a low tone means 'four'; with a rising tone, it means 'colour'. Thai is not written in Roman script but using an alphabet derived from Khmer. The Romanization given below is only intended to help in pronouncing Thai words. There is no accepted method of Romanization and some of the sounds in Thai cannot be accurately reproduced using Roman script.

Polite particles
At the end of sentences males use the polite particle *krúp*, and females, *kâ* or *ká*.

Learning Thai
The list of words and phrases below is only very rudimentary. For anyone serious about learning Thai it is best to buy a dedicated Thai language text book or to enrol on a Thai course. Recommended among the various 'teach yourself Thai' books is Somsong Buasai and David Smyth's *Thai in a Week,* Hodder & Stoughton: London (1990). A useful mini-dictionary is the Hugo *Thai phrase book* (1990). For those interested in learning to read and write Thai, the best 'teach yourself' course is the *Linguaphone* course.

General words and phrases

Yes/no	*chái/mâi chái, or krúp (kâ)/mâi krúp (kâ)*
Thank you/no thank you	*kòrp-kOOn/mâi ao kòrp-kOOn*
Hello, good morning, goodbye	*sa-wùt dee krúp(kâ)*
What is your name? My name is …	*koon chêu a-rai krúp (kâ)? Pom chêu …*
Excuse me, sorry!	*kor-tôht krúp(kâ)*
Can/do you speak English?	*KOON pôot pah-sah ung-grìt*
a little, a bit	*nít-nòy*
Where's the …?	*yòo têe-nai …?*
How much is …?	*tâo-rài …?*
Pardon?	*a-rai ná?*
I don't understand	*pom (chún) mâi kao jái*
How are you?	*mâi sa-bai*
Not very well	*sa-bai dee mái?*

At hotels

What is the charge each night?	*kâh hôrng wun la tâo-rài?*
Is the room air conditioned?	*hôrng dtìt air reu bplào?*
Can I see the room first please?	*kor doo hôrng gòrn dâi mái?*
Does the room have hot water?	*hôrng mii náhm rórn mái?*
Does the room have a bathroom?	*hôrng mii hôrng náhm mái?*
Can I have the bill please?	*kor bin nòy dâi mái?*

Travelling

Where is the train station?	*sa-tahn-nee rót fai yòo têe-nai?*
Where is the bus station?	*sa-tahn-nee rót may yòo têe-nai?*
How much to go to ...?	*bpai ... tâo-rài?*
That's expensive	*pairng bpai nòy*
What time does the bus/train leave for ...?	*rót may/rót fai bpai ...òrk gèe mohng?*
Is it far?	*glai mái?*
Turn left/turn right	*lée-o sái / lée-o kwah*
Go straight on	*ler-ee bpai èek*
It's straight ahead	*yòo dtrong nâh*

At restaurants

Can I see a menu?	*kor doo may-noo nòy?*
Can I have ...?/ I would like ...?	*kor ...*
Is it very (hot) spicy?	*pèt mâhk mái?*
I am hungry	*pom (chún) hew*
breakfast	*ah-hahn cháo*
lunch	*ah-hahn glanhg wun*

Time and days

in the morning	*dtorn cháo*	Monday	*wun jun*
in the afternoon	*dtorn bài*	Tuesday	*wun ung-kahn*
in the evening	*dtorn yen*	Wednesday	*wun pÓOt*
today	*wun née*	Thursday	*wun pá-réu-hùt*
tomorrow	*prÔOng née*	Friday	*wun sÒOk*
yesterday	*mêu-a wahn née*	Saturday	*wun sao*
		Sunday	*wun ah-tít*

Numbers

1	*nèung*	20	*yêe-sìp*
2	*sorng*	21	*yêe-sìp-et*
3	*sahm*	22	*yêe-sìp-sorng... etc*
4	*sèe*	30	*sahm-sìp*
5	*hâa*	100	*(nèung) róy*
6	*hòk*	101	*(nèung) róy-nèung*
7	*jèt*	150	*(nèung) róy-hâh-sìp*
8	*bpàirt*	200	*sorng róy ... etc*
9	*gâo*	1000	*(nèung) pun*
10	*sìp*	10,000	*mèun*
11	*sìp-et*	100,000	*sairn*
12	*sìp-sorng ... etc*	1,000,000	*láhn*

Basic vocabulary

airport	*a-nahm bin*	beach	*hàht*
bank	*ta-nah-kahn*	beautiful	*oo-ay*
bathroom	*hôrng náhm*	big	*yài*

boat	*reu-a*	medicine	*yah*
bus	*ót may*	open	*bpèrt*
bus station	*sa-tah-nee rót may*	police	*dtum-ròo-ut*
buy	*séu*	police station	*sa-tah-nee, dtum-ròo-ut*
chemist	*ráhn kai yah*	post office	*bprai-sa-nee*
clean	*sa-àht*	restaurant	*ráhn ah-hahn*
closed	*bpìt*	road	*thanon*
cold	*yen*	room	*hôrng*
day	*wun*	shop	*ráhn*
delicious	*a-ròy*	sick (ill)	*mâi sa-bai*
dirty	*sòk-ga-bpròk*	silk	*mai*
doctor	*mor*	small	*lék*
eat	*gin (kâo)*	stop	*yÒOt*
embassy	*sa-tahn tôot*	taxi	*táirk-sêe*
excellent	*yêe-um*	that	*nún*
expensive	*pairng*	this	*née*
food	*ah-hahn*	ticket	*dtoo-a*
fruit	*pon-la-mái*	toilet	*hôrng náhm*
hospital	*rohng pa-yah-bahn*	town	*meu-ung*
hot (temp)	*rórn*	train station	*sa-tah-nee rót fai*
hot (spicy)	*pèt*	very	*mâhk*
hotel	*rôhng rairm*	water	*náhm*
island	*gòr*	what	*a-rai*
market	*dta-làht*		

Glossary

A

Amitabha the Buddha of the Past (see Avalokitsvara)

Amulet protective medallion

Arhat a person who has perfected himself; images of former monks are sometimes carved into arhat

Avadana Buddhist narrative, telling of the deeds of saintly souls

Avalokitsvara also known as Amitabha and Lokeshvara, the name literally means 'World Lord'; he is the compassionate male Bodhisattva, the saviour of Mahayana Buddhism, and represents the central force of creation in the universe; usually portrayed with a lotus and water flask

B

Bai sema boundary stones marking consecrated ground around a Buddhist bot

Ban village; shortened from muban

Baray man-made lake or reservoir

Bhikku Buddhist monk

Bodhi the tree under which the Buddha achieved enlightenment (*Ficus religiosa*)

Bodhisattva a future Buddha. In Mahayana Buddhism, someone who has attained enlightenment, but who postpones nirvana to help others reach it.

Bor Kor Sor (BKS) Government bus terminal

Bot Buddhist ordination hall, of rectangular plan, identifiable by the boundary stones placed around it; an abbreviation of ubosoth

Brahma the Creator, one of the gods of the Hindu trinity, usually represented with four faces, and often mounted on a hamsa

Brahmin a Hindu priest

Bun to make merit

C

Caryatid elephants, often used as buttressing decorations

Celadon pottery ware with blue/green to grey glaze

Chakri the current royal dynasty in Thailand. They have reigned since 1782

Chao title for Lao and Thai kings

Chat honorific umbrella or royal multi-tiered parasol

Chedi from the Sanskrit *cetiya* (Pali, *caitya*), meaning memorial. Usually a religious monument (often bell-shaped), containing relics of the Buddha or other holy remains. Used interchangeably with stupa

Chofa 'sky tassel' on the roof of wat buildings

D

Deva a Hindu-derived male god

Devata a Hindu-derived goddess

Dharma the Buddhist law

Dvarapala guardian figure, usually placed at the entrance to a temple

G

Ganesh elephant-headed son of Siva

Garuda mythical divine bird, with predatory beak and claws, and human body; the king of birds, enemy of naga and mount of Vishnu

Gautama the historic Buddha

Geomancy the art of divination by lines and figures

Gopura crowned or covered gate, entrance to a religious area

H

Hamsa sacred goose, Brahma's mount; in Buddhism represents the flight of the doctrine

Hang yaaw long-tailed boat, used on canals

Harmika box-like part of a Burmese stupa that often acts as a reliquary casket

Hinayana 'Lesser Vehicle', major Buddhist sect in Southeast Asia, usually termed Theravada Buddhism

Hong swan

Hor kong a pavilion built on stilts, where the monastery drum is kept

Hor takang bell tower

Hor tray/trai library where manuscripts are stored in a Thai monastery

Hti 'umbrella' surmounting Burmese temples, often encrusted with jewels

---

I

Indra the Vedic god of the heavens, weather and war

J

Jataka(s) the birth stories of the Buddha; they normally number 547, although an additional three were added in Burma for reasons of symmetry in mural painting and sculpture. The last 10 are the most important

---

K

Kala (makara) literally 'death' or 'black'; a demon ordered to consume itself, often sculpted with grinning face and bulging eyes over entranceway to act as a door guardian; also known as kirtamukha

Kathin/krathin a one-month period during the eighth lunar month, when lay people present new robes and other gifts to monks

Ketumula flame-like motif above the Buddha head

Khao mountain

Kinaree half-human, half-bird, usually depicted as a heavenly musician

Krating wild bull, most commonly seen on bottles of *Red Bull* (Krating Daeng) drink

Krishna incarnation of Vishnu

Kuti living quarters of Buddhist monks in a monastery complex

---

L

Laem cape (as in bay)

Lakhon traditional Thai classical music

Lak muang city pillar

Linga phallic symbol and one of the forms of Siva. Embedded in a pedestal, shaped to allow drainage of lustral water poured over it; the linga typically has a succession of cross sections: from square at the base, through octagonal, to round. These symbolize, in order, the trinity of Brahma, Vishnu and Siva

Lintel a load-bearing stone spanning a doorway; often heavily carved

---

M

Mahabharata a Hindu epic text, written about 2000 years ago

Mahayana 'Greater Vehicle', Buddhist sect

Maitreya the future Buddha

Makara a mythological aquatic reptile, somewhat like a crocodile and sometimes with an elephant's trunk; often found along with the *kala* framing doorways

Mandala a focus for meditation; a representation of the cosmos

Mara personification of evil and tempter of the Buddha

Matmii Northeastern Thai cotton ikat

Meru sacred or cosmic mountain at the centre of the world in Hindu-Buddhist cosmology; home of the gods.

Mondop from the sanskrit, *mandapa*. A cube-shaped building, often topped with a cone-like structure, used to contain an object of worship like a footprint of the Buddha

Muban village, usually shortened to ban

Mudra symbolic gesture of the hands of the Buddha

N

Naga benevolent mythical water serpent, enemy of Garuda

Naga makara fusion of naga and makara

Nalagiri the elephant let loose to attack the Buddha, who calmed him

Namtok waterfall

Nandi/nandin bull, mount of Siva

Nang thalung shadow play/puppets

Nikhom resettlement village

Nirvana release from the cycle of suffering in Buddhist belief; 'enlightenment'

P

Pa kama Lao men's all-purpose cloth, usually woven with checked pattern

paddy/padi unhulled rice

Pali sacred language of Theravada Buddhism

Parvati consort of Siva

Pha sin tubular bit of cloth, similar to sarong

Phi spirit

Phnom/phanom Khmer for hill/mountain

Phra sinh see pha sin

Pradaksina pilgrims' clockwise circumambulation of holy structure

Prah sacred

Prang form of stupa built in Khmer style, shaped like a corncob

Prasada stepped pyramid (see prasat)

Prasat residence of a king or of the gods (sanctuary tower), from the Indian prasada

Q

Quan Am Chinese goddess of mercy

R

Rai unit of measurement, 1 ha = 6.25 rai

Rama incarnation of Vishnu, hero of the Indian epic, the *Ramayana*

Ramakien Thai version of the *Ramayana*

Ramayana Hindu romantic epic, known as *Ramakien* in Thailand

S

Saamlor three-wheeled bicycle taxi

Sakyamuni the historic Buddha

Sal the Indian sal tree (*Shorea robusta*), under which the historic Buddha was born

Sala open pavilion

Sangha the Buddhist order of monks

Sawankhalok type of ceramic

Singha mythical guardian lion

Siva the Destroyer, one of the three gods of the Hindu trinity

Sofa see dok sofa

Songthaew 'two rows': pick-up truck with benches along either side

Sravasti the miracle at Sravasti, the Buddha subdues the heretics in front of a mango tree

Stele inscribed stone panel

Stucco plaster, often heavily moulded

Stupa chedi

T

Talaat market

Tambon a commune of villages

Tam bun see bun

Tavatimsa heaven of the 33 gods, at the summit of Mount Meru

Tazaungs small pavilions, found within Burmese temple complexes

Tham cave

Thanon street in Thai

That shrine housing Buddhist relics, an edifice commemorating the Buddha's life or the funerary temple for royalty

Thein Burmese ordination hall

Theravada 'Way of the Elders'; major Buddhist sect, also known as Hinayana Buddhism ('Lesser Vehicle')

Traiphum the three worlds of Buddhist cosmology – heaven, hell and earth

Trimurti Hindu trinity of gods: Brahma, the Creator, Vishnu the Preserver, Siva the Destroyer

Tripitaka Theravada Buddhism's Pali canon

U

Ubosoth see bot

Urna the dot or curl on the Buddha's forehead

Usnisa the Buddha's top knot or 'wisdom bump',

V

Vahana a mythical beast, upon which a deva or god rides

Viharn an assembly hall in a Buddhist monastery; may hold Buddha images

Vishnu the Protector, one of the gods of the Hindu trinity

W

Wai Thai greeting, with hands held together at chin height as if in prayer

Wat Buddhist 'monastery'

Z

Zayat prayer pavilion found in Burmese temple complexes

Zedi Burmese term for a stupa

Food glossary → *See also Thai dishes, opposite.*

a-haan food
ba-mii egg noodles
bia beer
chaa tea
check bin/bill cheque
chorn spoon
gaeng curry
gaeng chud soup
jaan plate
kaafae (ron) coffee (hot)
kaew glass
kai chicken
kap klaem snacks to be eaten when drinking
khaaw/khao rice
khaaw niaw sticky rice
khaaw tom rice gruel
khai egg
khai dao fried egg
khanom sweet, dessert or cake
khanom cake cake
khanom pang bread
khanom pang ping toast
khing ginger
khuan scramble
khuat bottle
kin to eat

kleua salt
krueng kieng side dishes
kung crab
kwaytio noodle soup, white noodles
laap pa raw fish crushed into a paste, marinated in lemon juice and mixed with chopped mint, chilli and rice grains
laap sin raw meat dish, see above
lao liquor
man root vegetable
man farang potatoes
manaaw lemon
mekong a Thai whisky
mit knife
muu pork
nam chaa tea
nam kheng ice
nam kuat bottled water
nam manaaw soda lime soda
nam plaa fish sauce
nam plaa prik fish sauce with chilli
nam plaaw plain water

nam som orange juice
nam taan sugar
nam tom boiled water
nom milk
nua meat (usually beef)
phak vegetables
phat to stir fry
phet hot (chilli)
phon lamai fruit
pla fish
priaw sour
priaw waan sweet and sour
prik hot chilli
raan a-haan restaurant
ratnaa in gravy
rawn hot (temperature)
sa-te satay
sorm fork
talaat market
thao mai luai morning glory
thua nut/bean
tom to boil
tort to deep fry
waan sweet
yam salad
yen cold

Thai dishes

It is impossible to provide a comprehensive list of Thai dishes. However (and at the risk of offending connoisseurs by omitting their favourites), popular dishes include:

Soups (*gaeng chud*)
Kaeng juut bean curd and vegetable soup, non-spicy

Khaaw tom rice soup with egg and pork (a breakfast dish) or chicken, fish or prawn. It is said that it can cure fevers and other illnesses. Probably best for a hangover.

Kwaytio Chinese noodle soup served with a variety of additional ingredients, often available from roadside stalls and from smaller restaurants – mostly served up until lunchtime.

Tom ka kai chicken in coconut milk with laos (loas, or ka, is an exotic spice)

Tom yam kung hot and sour prawn soup spiced with lemon grass, coriander and chillies

Rice-based dishes
Single-dish meals served at roadside stalls and in many restaurants (especially cheaper ones).

Khaaw gaeng curry and rice

Khaaw man kai rice with chicken

Khaaw mu daeng rice with red pork

Khaaw naa pet rice with duck

Khaaw phat kai/mu/kung fried rice with chicken/pork/prawn

Noodle-based dishes
Ba-mii haeng wheat noodles served with pork and vegetables

Khaaw soi a form of *Kwaytio* with egg noodles in a curry broth

Kwaytio haeng wide noodles served with pork and vegetables

Mee krop Thai crisp-fried noodles

Phak sii-u noodles fried with egg, vegetables and meat/prawns

Phat thai Thai fried noodles

Curries (*gaeng*)
Gaeng khiaw waan kai/nua/phet/pla green chicken/beef/duck/fish curry (the colour is due to the large number of whole green chillies pounded to make the paste that forms the base of this very hot curry)

Gaeng mussaman Muslim beef curry served with potatoes

Gaeng phanaeng chicken/beef curry

Gaeng phet kai/nua hot chicken/ beef curry

Gaeng plaa duk catfish curry

Meat dishes
Kai/mu/nua phat kapow fried meat with basil and chillies

Kai/nua phat prik fried chicken/beef with chillies

Kai tort Thai fried chicken

Kai tua chicken in peanut sauce

Kai yang garlic chicken

Laap chopped (once raw, now frequently cooked) meat with herbs and spices

Mu waan sweet pork

Nua priaw waan sweet and sour beef

Priao wan sweet and sour pork with vegetables

Seafood
Haw mok steamed fish curry

Luuk ciin fishballs

Plaa nerng steamed fish

Plaa pao grilled fish

Plaa priaw waan whole fried fish with ginger sauce

Plaa too tort Thai fried fish

Thotman plaa fried curried fish cakes

Salads (*yam*)
Som tam green papaya salad with tomatoes, chillies, garlic, chopped dried shrimps and lemon (can be extremely hot)

Yam nua Thai beef salad

Vegetables
Phak phat ruam mit mixed fried vegetables

Sweets (*kanom*)
Kanom mo kaeng baked custard squares
Khaaw niaw mamuang sticky rice and
mango (a seasonal favourite)
Khaaw niaw sankhayaa sticky rice and
custard
Kluay buat chee bananas in coconut milk
Kluay tort Thai fried bananas
Leenchee loi mek chilled lychees in custard

Fruits
Chomphu rose apple
Khanun jackfruit. Jan-Jun
Kluay banana. Year round
Lamyai longan; thin brown shell with
translucent fruit similar to lychee. Jun-Aug

Lamut sapodilla
Linchi lychee. Apr-Jun
Majeung star apple
Makham wan tamarind. Dec-Feb
Malakho papaya. Year round
Mamuang mango. Mar-Jun
Manaaw lime. Year round
Mang khud mangosteen. Apr-Sep
Maprao coconut. Year round
Ngo rambutan. May-Sep
Noi na custard (or sugar) apple. Jun-Sep
Sapparot pineapple. Apr-Jun, Dec-Jan
Som orange. Year round
Som o pomelo. Aug-Nov
Taeng mo watermelon. Oct-Mar
Thurian durian. May-Aug

Index

Titles available in the Footprint *Focus* range

Latin America	UK RRP	US RRP
Bahia & Salvador	£7.99	$11.95
Brazilian Amazon	£7.99	$11.95
Brazilian Pantanal	£6.99	$9.95
Buenos Aires & Pampas	£7.99	$11.95
Cartagena & Caribbean Coast	£7.99	$11.95
Costa Rica	£8.99	$12.95
Cuzco, La Paz & Lake Titicaca	£8.99	$12.95
El Salvador	£5.99	$8.95
Guadalajara & Pacific Coast	£6.99	$9.95
Guatemala	£8.99	$12.95
Guyana, Guyane & Suriname	£5.99	$8.95
Havana	£6.99	$9.95
Honduras	£7.99	$11.95
Nicaragua	£7.99	$11.95
Northeast Argentina & Uruguay	£8.99	$12.95
Paraguay	£5.99	$8.95
Quito & Galápagos Islands	£7.99	$11.95
Recife & Northeast Brazil	£7.99	$11.95
Rio de Janeiro	£8.99	$12.95
São Paulo	£5.99	$8.95
Uruguay	£6.99	$9.95
Venezuela	£8.99	$12.95
Yucatán Peninsula	£6.99	$9.95

Asia	UK RRP	US RRP
Angkor Wat	£5.99	$8.95
Bali & Lombok	£8.99	$12.95
Chennai & Tamil Nadu	£8.99	$12.95
Chiang Mai & Northern Thailand	£7.99	$11.95
Goa	£6.99	$9.95
Gulf of Thailand	£8.99	$12.95
Hanoi & Northern Vietnam	£8.99	$12.95
Ho Chi Minh City & Mekong Delta	£7.99	$11.95
Java	£7.99	$11.95
Kerala	£7.99	$11.95
Kolkata & West Bengal	£5.99	$8.95
Mumbai & Gujarat	£8.99	$12.95

Africa & Middle East	UK RRP	US RRP
Beirut	£6.99	$9.95
Cairo & Nile Delta	£8.99	$12.95
Damascus	£5.99	$8.95
Durban & KwaZulu Natal	£8.99	$12.95
Fès & Northern Morocco	£8.99	$12.95
Jerusalem	£8.99	$12.95
Johannesburg & Kruger National Park	£7.99	$11.95
Kenya's Beaches	£8.99	$12.95
Kilimanjaro & Northern Tanzania	£8.99	$12.95
Luxor to Aswan	£8.99	$12.95
Nairobi & Rift Valley	£7.99	$11.95
Red Sea & Sinai	£7.99	$11.95
Zanzibar & Pemba	£7.99	$11.95

Europe	UK RRP	US RRP
Bilbao & Basque Region	£6.99	$9.95
Brittany West Coast	£7.99	$11.95
Cádiz & Costa de la Luz	£6.99	$9.95
Granada & Sierra Nevada	£6.99	$9.95
Languedoc: Carcassonne to Montpellier	£7.99	$11.95
Málaga	£5.99	$8.95
Marseille & Western Provence	£7.99	$11.95
Orkney & Shetland Islands	£5.99	$8.95
Santander & Picos de Europa	£7.99	$11.95
Sardinia: Alghero & the North	£7.99	$11.95
Sardinia: Cagliari & the South	£7.99	$11.95
Seville	£5.99	$8.95
Sicily: Palermo & the Northwest	£7.99	$11.95
Sicily: Catania & the Southeast	£7.99	$11.95
Siena & Southern Tuscany	£7.99	$11.95
Sorrento, Capri & Amalfi Coast	£6.99	$9.95
Skye & Outer Hebrides	£6.99	$9.95
Verona & Lake Garda	£7.99	$11.95

North America	UK RRP	US RRP
Vancouver & Rockies	£8.99	$12.95

Australasia	UK RRP	US RRP
Brisbane & Queensland	£8.99	$12.95
Perth	£7.99	$11.95

For the latest books, e-books and a wealth of travel information, visit us at: www.footprinttravelguides.com.

Join us on facebook for the latest travel news, product releases, offers and amazing competitions: www.facebook.com/footprintbooks.